Faith Based Statements on Climate Change

Contents

INTERFAITH ORGANIZATIONS

REFERENCES

Anglicans, Episcopalians issue statement on climate justice, form commitments

(From ENS, Episcopal News Service)

(See also Episcopalian statement on page 27.)

By Lynette Wilson, December 13, 2010

As Anglicans and Episcopalians met last week in the Dominican Republic to share their stories and organize around issues of climate justice, in Panama heavy rains and floods killed at least 10 people, displaced 4,700 more, and forced the first-ever weather-related closure of the Panama Canal.

"While we are here for the conference on climate justice, in Panama people are being evacuated out of areas that are being flooded," said Bishop Julio Murray of the Episcopal Church of Panama Dec. 9, in an interview with ENS. "The groups that are mostly affected are the indigenous groups that live in the area of Alto Bayano . . . it is the first time in my lifetime that the Panama Canal has had to suspend traffic ... this is an example of what happens when water levels rise in rapid ways."

More than 30 people—mostly Anglicans and Episcopalians and a few ecumenical seminarians—from Cuba, the United States, Ecuador, Panama, Colombia, Haiti, Mexico, Brazil, Guatemala and the Dominican Republic met Dec. 7 - 10 at the Bishop Kellogg Center in San Pedro de Macorís, east of the capital Santo Domingo, to explore intersection between poverty and climate change and frame the conversation in terms of "climate justice." The meeting was convened by Bishop Marc Andrus of the Episcopal Diocese of California, and Bishop Naudal Gomes, Diocese of Curitiba, Brazil.

"It was just our two dioceses, California and Curitiba, coming together to work on climate justice during this time and it was like a magnet—all these dioceses, I think 10, two provinces in addition to the Episcopal Church have gathered together here to tell their stories," said Andrus in a Dec. 10 interview with ENS.

"We've written a statement that expresses where we came from and what we hope," he said. "We are creating the beginning of a network ... we are committed to each other and welcoming more partners to this network for climate justice."

Throughout the four-day gathering, attendees shared personal accounts of their witness to climate injustice and creative responses by dioceses, communities and individuals. At the close of the gathering, building on the week's presentations, discussions and a four-hour brainstorming session aimed at creating action points, attending bishops wrote a draft statement recognizing the urgency of climate change and the need to act. By vote, attendees winnowed down more than 50 action points, committing to five as a basis for collaboration and action.

The draft statement begins, "We are a group of Anglican Episcopals from Latin America, the Caribbean, and the United States who feel the urgency of addressing climate justice at this time in the world we serve."

It ends with the commitments: to develop an energy fund for carbon reduction; to teach climate justice at all ages and levels of the church; to stay connected as a consortium for climate justice; to support outside initiatives aimed at emissions reduction, to provide support for people directly affected by deforestation and people living in forested areas, and to promote food sovereignty; and support for training missionaries from the global south to share stories of how climate change is directly affecting life in the developing world to people in the United States, who may not understand its direct effects.

Michael Schut, economic and environmental affairs officer for the Episcopal Church, addressed the last point in an interview with ENS Dec. 10, when he said the level of climate change – related suffering in the developing world doesn't resonate with most people in the United States.

"Meeting people from around the world with a very different perspective helps me at least understand a little bit more about what it's like to live in a different context," he said.

The Episcopal-Anglican gathering coincided with the second week of the U.N. Climate Change Conference in Cancun, Mexico, during which delegates from 193 countries developed a new global framework to help developing nations curb their carbon output and cope with climate change. The Cancun talks stopped short of coming up with an agreement to replace the Kyoto Protocol, which expires in 2012. The protocol commits 37 industrialized nations to cut greenhouse gas emissions by 20 percent (below 1990 levels) by 2020 and 80 percent by 2050.

Although there were many environmental action groups on the ground in Cancun, the Episcopal-Anglican gathering was the only known religious gathering of its kind taking place at the same time, and was remarkable in that it brought churches from the global south and the north together.

This gathering has been a chance for all the churches from all parts of America—northern, southern, central—and the Caribbean to get together to discuss climate justice issues and to share ideas "about the things that we can do together, things that cannot be accomplished alone," Gomes told ENS, speaking in Portuguese through a translator.

Bishop Griselda Delgado Del Carpio of the Episcopal Church of Cuba shared how a 2,000 square-foot garden started by La Iglesia Santa Maria Virgen in Itabo, Cuba, grew into a community-wide project. A representative from Oxfam talked specifically about the connection between the Dominican Republic's changing climate and deforestation.

The Rev. Luiz Carlos Gabas, of Brazil, described how Brazil's "landless people's movement," which started in the early 1960s, became one of the world's largest grassroots movements. Gabas, who has been active in the movement, told how its original aim of access to land and agrarian reform has changed over the years from fighting large landowners to multi-national agribusiness biotechnology companies.

"There was a time when the struggle was easier. We could see the enemy, the landowner, but that has changed," said Gabas, as translated from Portuguese. "Now it has changed, the landlords are international and transnational agribusiness companies that influence what happens in the country … price controls in the consumer market … they want to control seed production."

The agribusiness companies have introduced monoculture and their own production methods. The remaining large private landowners have partnered with agribusiness, creating an uneven struggle, he said.

The grassroots movement now works to train people to be part of the struggle by educating them about social and Brazilian history, training agriculture students and teachers to work in rural areas. As a result, Brazilian farmers are rediscovering and saving native seeds and the government supports establishing a seed bank, Gabas added.

On Dec. 8, Bishop Armando Guerra of the Episcopal Church of Guatemala said that in his country's native language, "Guatemala means land of the trees," yet many of his country's climate-related problems are exacerbated by deforestation; Guatemala loses 73,000 hectares of forest a year, he said.

Guatemala's 14 million people emit 1 ton of carbon dioxide per person per year, in contrast to the 310 million Americans who emit 20.5 tons of carbon dioxide per person. Still, he explained, Guatemalans are contributing to climate change.

"Although Guatemala doesn't affect that much, the people can do things to stop the continuation of climate change," Guerra said, as translated from Spanish. "They can't use that it's a global problem as an excuse. They can't just stand by and not do anything."

Climate change is affecting all levels of society, Guerra said. He called the church to respond.

In the last 10 years, Guerra explained, hurricanes and tropical storms have increased in frequency and severity, and are beginning to take a psychological toll on the people most affected. Climate change has directly affected Guatemala's development and people's ability to find work, feed themselves and pay for life's necessities. As a result young people are leaving school early, turning to prostitution and other illicit business, and there has been a mass migration—a situation that is only going to get worse, he said.

The church, Guerra said, just like average people, thinks that "someone else" is responsible for climate change.

"This situation brings a problem to Christian churches that have to decide what to do . . . the churches also have that same thought, that someone else is causing the problem . . . and the church always blames the political, social and economic areas of life and doesn't take responsibility for it . . . but if the churches are part of the problem, they also have to be part of the solution," he said.

In addition to the Anglicans and Episcopalians attending the gathering, a small group of students taking Professor Willis Jenkins's environmental theology class at Yale Divinity School, were in attendance.

"As part of that class, I emphasize that what environmental theologies should do to become effective is to figure out how to make difficult problems significant with the lived experience of faith communities," Jenkins said.

Anglican

The Yale School of Forestry and Environmental Studies offers a joint degree program with Berkeley Divinity School—an Episcopal Church – affiliate seminary that has been in collaboration with Yale Divinity School since 1971—that allows students to explore the "role of environment through an environmental lens."

The Yale program is unusual, Jenkins said, but is catching on at other universities and seminaries.

The church has to figure out how to "make issues of climate change as a way to act and pursue the mission of God," Jenkins said.

The Episcopal Church, through its General Convention, has adopted various resolutions related to the environment, including memorializing the Genesis Covenant, "a multi-faith effort to engage national faith communities in a single and significant course of action to reduce the damaging effects of climate change."

Lynette Wilson is an ENS staff writer.

A Southern Baptist Declaration on the Environment and Climate Change

This declaration on climate change was signed by over 40 Southern Baptist leaders in March, 2008. The Southern Baptist Convention previously questioned the degree of human influence on global warming. This declaration calls for taking action against climate change. http://www.cfr.org/religion-and-politics/southern-baptist-declaration-environment-climate-change/p15847

Preamble

Southern Baptists have always been a confessional people, giving testimony to our beliefs, which are based upon the doctrines found in God's inerrant word—the Holy Bible. As the dawning of new ages has produced substantial challenges requiring a special word, Southern Baptist churches, associations and general bodies have often found it necessary to make declarations in order to define, express and defend beliefs. Though we do not regard this as a complete declaration on these issues, we believe this initiative finds itself consistent with our most cherished distinctives and rooted in historical precedent.

The preamble to the *Baptist Faith and Message 2000* (BFM 2000) declares: "Each generation of Christians bears the responsibility of guarding the treasury of truth that has been entrusted to us [2 Timothy 1:14]. Facing a new century, Southern Baptists must meet the demands and duties of the present hour. New challenges to faith appear in every age."

We recognize that God's great blessings on our denomination bestow upon us a great responsibility to offer a biblically-based, moral witness that can help shape individual behavior, private sector behavior and public policy. Conversations like this one demand our voice in order to fulfill our calling to engage the culture as a relevant body of believers. Southern Baptists have always championed faith's challenges, and we now perpetuate our heritage through this initiative.

We are proud of our deep and lasting commitments to moral issues like the sanctity of human life and biblical definitions of marriage. We will never compromise our convictions nor attenuate our advocacy on these matters, which constitute the most pressing moral issues of our day. However, we are not a single-issue body. We also offer moral witness in other venues and on many issues. We seek to be true to our calling as Christian leaders, but above all, faithful to Jesus Christ our Lord. Therefore, our attention goes to whatever issues our faith requires us to address.

We have recently engaged in study, reflection and prayer related to the challenges presented by environmental and climate change issues. These things have not always been treated with pressing concern as major issues. Indeed, some of us have required considerable convincing before becoming persuaded that these are real problems that deserve our attention. But now we have seen and heard enough to be persuaded that these issues are among the current era's challenges that require a unified moral voice.

We believe our current denominational engagement with these issues have often been too timid, failing to produce a unified moral voice. Our cautious response to these issues in the face of mounting evidence may be seen by the world as uncaring, reckless and ill-informed. We can do better. To abandon these issues to the secular world is to shirk from our responsibility to be salt and light. The time for timidity regarding God's creation is no more.

Therefore, we offer these four statements for consideration, beginning with our fellow Southern Baptists, and urge all to follow by taking appropriate actions. May we find ourselves united as we contend for the faith that was delivered to the saints once for all. *Laus Deo!*

Statement 1

Humans Must Care for Creation and Take Responsibility for Our Contributions to Environmental Degradation.

There is undeniable evidence that the earth—wildlife, water, land and air—can be damaged by human activity, and that people suffer as a result. When this happens, it is especially egregious because creation serves as revelation of God's presence, majesty and provision. Though not every person will physically hear God's revelation found in Scripture, all people have access to God's cosmic revelation: the heavens, the waters, natural order, the beauty of nature (Psalm 19; Romans 1). We believe that human activity is mixed in its impact on creation—sometimes productive and caring, but often reckless, preventable and sinful.

God's command to tend and keep the earth (Genesis 2) did not pass away with the fall of man; we are still responsible. Lack of concern and failure to act prudently on the part of Christ followers reflects poorly to the rest of the world. Therefore, we humbly take responsibility for the damage that we have done to God's cosmic revelation and pledge to take an unwavering stand to preserve and protect the creation over which we have been given responsibility by Almighty God Himself.

Statement 2

It Is Prudent to Address Global Climate Change.

We recognize that we do not have any special revelation to guide us about whether global warming is occurring and, if it is occurring, whether people are causing it. We are looking at the same evidence unfolding over time that other people are seeing.

We recognize that we do not have special training as scientists to allow us to assess the validity of climate science. We understand that all human enterprises are fraught with pride, bias, ignorance and uncertainty.

We recognize that if consensus means unanimity, there is not a consensus regarding the anthropogenic nature of climate change or the severity of the problem. There is general agreement among those engaged with this issue in the scientific community. A minority of sincere and respected scientists offer alternate causes for global climate change other than deforestation and the burning of fossil fuels.

We recognize that Christians are not united around either the scientific explanations for global warming or policies designed to slow it down. Unlike abortion and respect for the biblical definition of marriage, this is an issue where Christians may find themselves in justified disagreement about both the problem and its solutions.

Yet, even in the absence of perfect knowledge or unanimity, we have to make informed decisions about the future. This will mean we have to take a position of prudence based partly on science that is inevitably changing. We do not believe unanimity is necessary for prudent action. We can make wise decisions even in the absence of infallible evidence.

Though the claims of science are neither infallible nor unanimous, they are substantial and cannot be dismissed out of hand on either scientific or theological grounds. Therefore, in the face of intense concern and guided by the biblical principle of creation stewardship, we resolve to engage this issue without any further lingering over the basic reality of the problem or our responsibility to address it. Humans must be proactive and take responsibility for our contributions to climate change—however great or small.

Statement 3

Christian Moral Convictions and Our Southern Baptist Doctrines Demand Our Environmental Stewardship.

While we cannot here review the full range of relevant Christian convictions and Baptist doctrines related to care of the creation, we emphasize the following points:

- We must care about environmental and climate issues because of our love for God—"the Creator, Redeemer, Preserver and Ruler of the Universe" (BFM 2000)—through whom and for whom the creation was made. This is not our world, it is God's. Therefore, any damage we do to this world is an offense against God Himself (Gen. 1; Ps. 24; Col. 1:16). We share God's concern for the abuse of His creation.

- We must care about environmental issues because of our commitment to God's Holy and inerrant Word, which is "the supreme standard by which all human conduct, creeds and religious opinions should be tried" (BFM 2000). Within these Scriptures we are reminded that when God made mankind, He commissioned us to exercise stewardship over the earth and its creatures (Gen. 1:26-28). **Therefore, our motivation for facing failures to exercise proper stewardship is not primarily political, social or economic—it is primarily biblical.**

- We must care about environmental and climate issues because we are called to love our neighbors, to do unto others as we would have them do unto us and to protect and care for the "least of these" (Mt. 22:34-40; Mt. 7:12; Mt. 25:31-46). The consequences of these problems will most likely hit the poor the hardest, in part because those areas likely to be significantly affected are in the world's poorest regions. Poor nations and individuals have fewer resources available to cope with major challenges and threats. Therefore, "we should work to provide for the orphaned, the needy ... [and] the helpless" (BFM 2000) through proper stewardship. Love of God, love of neighbor and Scripture's stewardship demands provide enough reason for Southern Baptists and Christians everywhere to respond to these problems with moral passion and concrete action.

Statement 4

It Is Time for Individuals, Churches, Communities and Governments to Act.

We affirm that "every Christian should seek to bring industry, government and society as a whole under the sway of the principles of righteousness, truth and brotherly love" (BFM 2000).

We realize that we cannot support some environmental issues as we offer a distinctively Christian voice in these arenas. For instance, we realize that what some call population control leads to evils like abortion. We now call on these environmentalists to reject these evils and accept the sanctity of every human person, both born and unborn.

We realize that simply affirming our God-given responsibility to care for the earth will likely produce no tangible or effective results. Therefore, we pledge to find ways to curb ecological degradation through promoting biblical stewardship habits and increasing awareness in our homes, businesses where we find influence, relationships with others and in our local churches. Many of our churches do not actively preach, promote or practice biblical creation care. We urge churches to begin doing so.

We realize that the primary impetus for prudent action must come from the will of the people, families and those in the private sector. Held to this standard of common good, action by government is often needed to assure the health and well-being of all people. We pledge, therefore, to give serious consideration to responsible policies that acceptably address the conditions set forth in this declaration.

Conclusion

We the undersigned, in accordance with our Christian moral convictions and Southern Baptist doctrines, pledge to act on the basis of the claims made in this document. We will not only teach the truths communicated here but also seek ways to implement the actions that follow from them. In the name of Jesus Christ our Lord, we urge all who read this declaration to join us in this effort. *Laus Deo!*

A Buddhist Declaration on Climate Change

From Website: Ecological Buddhism: A Buddhist Response to Global Warming [c. Sept. 2008]
http://www.ecobuddhism.org/bcp/all_content/buddhist_declaration/

The Declaration that follows presents to the world's media a unique spiritual view of climate change and our urgent responsibility to address the solutions. It emerged from the contributions of over 20 Buddhist teachers of all traditions to the book *A Buddhist Response to the Climate Emergency. The Time to Act is Now* was composed as a pan-Buddhist statement by Zen teacher Dr David Tetsuun Loy and senior Theravadin teacher Ven. Bhikkhu Bodhi with scientific input from Dr John Stanley. The Dalai Lama was the first to sign this Declaration. We invite all concerned members of the international Buddhist community to study the document and add their voice by co-signing it at the end of this page.

The Time to Act is Now

A Buddhist Declaration on Climate Change

Today we live in a time of great crisis, confronted by the gravest challenge that humanity has ever faced: the ecological consequences of our own collective karma. The scientific consensus is overwhelming: human activity is triggering environmental breakdown on a planetary scale. Global warming, in particular, is happening much faster than previously predicted, most obviously at the North Pole. For hundreds of thousands of years, the Arctic Ocean has been covered by an area of sea ice as large as Australia—but now this is melting rapidly. In 2007 the Intergovernmental Panel on Climate Change (IPCC) forecast that the Arctic might be free of summer sea ice by 2100. It is now apparent that this could occur within a decade or two. Greenland's vast ice-sheet is also melting more quickly than expected. The rise in sea level this century will be at least one meter—enough to flood many coastal cities and vital rice-growing areas such as the Mekong Delta in Vietnam.

Glaciers all over the world are receding quickly. If current economic policies continue, the glaciers of the Tibetan Plateau, source of the great rivers that provide water for billions of people in Asia, are likely to disappear by mid-century. Severe drought and crop failures are already affecting Australia and Northern China. Major reports—from the IPCC, United Nations, European Union, and International Union for Conservation of Nature—agree that, without a collective change of direction, dwindling supplies of water, food and other resources could create famine conditions, resource battles, and mass migration by mid-century—perhaps by 2030, according to the U.K.'s chief scientific advisor.

Global warming plays a major role in other ecological crises, including the loss of many plant and animal species that share this Earth with us. Oceanographers report that half the carbon released by burning fossil fuels has been absorbed by the oceans, increasing their acidity by about 30%. Acidification is disrupting calcification of shells and coral reefs, as well as threatening plankton growth, the source of the food chain for most life in the sea.

Eminent biologists and U.N. reports concur that "business-as-usual" will drive half of all species on Earth to extinction within this century. Collectively, we are violating the first precept—"do not harm living beings"—on the largest possible scale. And we cannot foresee the biological consequences for human life when so many species that invisibly contribute to our own well-being vanish from the planet.

Many scientists have concluded that the survival of human civilization is at stake. We have reached a critical juncture in our biological and social evolution. There has never been a more important time in history to bring the resources of Buddhism to bear on behalf of all living beings. The four noble truths provide a framework for diagnosing our current situation and formulating appropriate guidelines—because the threats and disasters we face ultimately stem from the human mind, and therefore require profound changes within our minds. If personal suffering stems from craving and ignorance—from the three poisons of greed, ill will, and delusion—the same applies to the suffering that afflicts us on a collective scale. Our ecological emergency is a larger version of the perennial human predicament. Both as individuals and as a species, we suffer from a sense of self that feels disconnected not only from other people but from the Earth itself. As Thich Nhat Hanh has said, "We are here to awaken from the illusion of our separateness." We need to wake up and realize that the Earth is our mother as well as our home—and in this case the umbilical cord binding us to her cannot be severed. When the Earth becomes sick, we become sick, because we are part of her.

Our present economic and technological relationships with the rest of the biosphere are unsustainable. To survive the rough transitions ahead, our lifestyles and expectations must change. This involves new habits as well as new values. The Buddhist teaching that the overall health of the individual and society depends upon inner well-being, and not merely upon economic indicators, helps us determine the personal and social changes we must make.

Individually, we must adopt behaviors that increase everyday ecological awareness and reduce our "carbon footprint." Those of us in the advanced economies need to retrofit and insulate our homes and workplaces for energy efficiency; lower thermostats in winter and raise them in summer; use high efficiency light bulbs and appliances; turn off unused electrical appliances; drive the most fuel-efficient cars possible, and reduce meat consumption in favor of a healthy, environmentally friendly, plant-based diet.

These personal activities will not by themselves be sufficient to avert future calamity. We must also make institutional changes, both technological and economic. We must "de-carbonize" our energy systems as quickly as feasible by replacing fossil fuels with renewable energy sources that are limitless, benign and harmonious with nature. We especially need to halt the construction of new coal plants, since coal is by far the most polluting and most dangerous source of atmospheric carbon. Wisely utilized, wind power, solar power, tidal power, and geothermal power can provide all the electricity that we require without damaging the biosphere. Since up to a quarter of world carbon emissions result from deforestation, we must reverse the destruction of forests, especially the vital rainforest belt where most species of plants and animals live.

It has recently become quite obvious that significant changes are also needed in the way our economic system is structured. Global warming is intimately related to the gargantuan quantities of energy that our industries devour to provide the levels of consumption that many of us have learned to expect. From a Buddhist perspective, a sane and sustainable economy would be governed by the principle of sufficiency: the key to happiness is contentment rather than an ever-increasing abundance of goods. The compulsion to consume more and more is an expression of craving, the very thing the Buddha pinpointed as the root cause of suffering.

Instead of an economy that emphasizes profit and requires perpetual growth to avoid collapse, we need to move together towards an economy that provides a satisfactory standard of living for everyone while allowing us to develop our full (including spiritual) potential in harmony with the biosphere that sustains and nurtures all beings, including future generations. If political leaders are unable to recognize the urgency of our global crisis, or unwilling to put the long-term good of humankind above the short-term benefit of fossil-fuel corporations, we may need to challenge them with sustained campaigns of citizen action.

Dr. James Hansen of NASA and other climatologists have recently defined the precise targets needed to prevent global warming from reaching catastrophic "tipping points." For human civilization to be sustainable, the safe level of carbon dioxide in the atmosphere is no more than 350 parts per million (ppm). This target has been endorsed by the Dalai Lama, along with other Nobel laureates and distinguished scientists. Our current situation is particularly worrisome in that the present level is already 387 ppm, and has been rising at 2 ppm per year. We are challenged not only to reduce carbon emissions, but also to remove large quantities of carbon gas already present in the atmosphere.

As signatories to this statement of Buddhist principles, we acknowledge the urgent challenge of climate change. We join with the Dalai Lama in endorsing the 350 ppm target. In accordance with Buddhist teachings, we accept our individual and collective responsibility to do whatever we can to meet this target, including (but not limited to) the personal and social responses outlined above.

We have a brief window of opportunity to take action, to preserve humanity from imminent disaster and to assist the survival of the many diverse and beautiful forms of life on Earth. Future generations, and the other species that share the biosphere with us, have no voice to ask for our compassion, wisdom, and leadership. We must listen to their silence. We must be their voice, too, and act on their behalf.

Tibetan Buddhist Statement on Climate Change

From Ecological Buddhism: A Buddhist Response to Global Warming [c. December, 2008]
website: http://www.ecobuddhism.org/index.php/bcp/all_content/3rd_pole/dl_wikileaks/

(The Dalai Lama is the leader of the Tibetan Buddhists.)

The Dalai Lama:

Focus Should Now Be on Climate Change, not Politics, in Tibet

The Dalai Lama has told US diplomats that the international community should focus on climate change rather than politics in Tibet because environmental problems were more urgent, secret American cables have revealed through *Wikileaks*.

The exiled Tibetan Buddhist spiritual leader told Timothy Roemer, the US ambassador to India, that the "political agenda should be sidelined for five to 10 years and the international community should shift its focus to climate change on the Tibetan plateau" during a meeting in Delhi last August.

"Melting glaciers, deforestation and increasingly polluted water from mining projects were problems that 'cannot wait,' but the Tibetans could wait five to 10 years for a political solution," he was reported as saying.

Though the Dalai Lama has frequently raised environmental issues, he has never publicly suggested that political questions take second place, nor spoken of any timescale with such precision.

Roemer speculated, in his cable to Washington reporting the meeting, that "the Dalai Lama's message may signal a broader shift in strategy to reframe the Tibet issue as an environmental concern."

The following endorsement from the Dalai Lama is also from the same website:

Ecological Buddhism: A Buddhist Response to Global Warming
http://www.ecobuddhism.org/bcp/all_content/350_hhdl/

We are honored to present here the Dalai Lama's official letter of endorsement of the 350 ppm target. Among the growing list of other international figures supporting this target are Nobel Laureate Archbishop Desmond Tutu, Indian environmental leader Dr. Vandana Shiva, Canadian biologist and broadcaster Dr.David Suzuki, Dr.Hermann Scheer, chairman of the World Council for Renewable Energy, and Sheila Watt-Cloutier, chairperson of the Inuit Circumpolar Council. It has been endorsed in a personal capacity by Dr Rajendra Pachauri, head of the IPCC. The world's leading climate economist Sir Nicholas Stern describes it as "a very sensible long-term target":

The Dalai Lama

Endorsement

Right now our greatest responsibility is to undo the damage done by the introduction of fossil carbon dioxide into the atmosphere and climate system during the rise of human civilization.

We know that we have already exceeded the 350 parts per million that is a safe level of carbon dioxide in the atmosphere. In doing so, we have ushered in a global climate crisis. This is evident from the frequent extreme weather events we witness around us, the unprecedented melting of the Arctic sea ice and of the great Tibetan glaciers at the Earth's _Third Pole_.

It is now urgent that we take corrective action to ensure a safe climate future for coming generations of human beings and other species. That can be established in perpetuity if we can reduce atmospheric carbon dioxide to 350 ppm. Buddhists, concerned people of the world and all people of good heart should be aware of this and act upon it.

December 20, 2008

The Vatican takes on climate change: it's cheaper to fix *now*

By Eric Bangeman

(from *Ars Technica*, 2011)

The Vatican Pontifical Academy of Sciences has just released a strongly worded report (PDF) on global climate change demanding in the strongest possible language that humans act decisively to avert a coming crisis. "We call on all people and nations to recognize the serious and potentially reversible impacts of global warming caused by the anthropogenic emissions of greenhouse gases and other pollutants," says the report. "If we want justice and peace, we must protect the habitat that sustains us."

The report was not authored by the Pontifical Academy itself; rather, the Vatican convened a group of scientists with relevant experience, along with a few Nobel Prize winners. The group's focus was on increasing evidence of glacier retreat, and the report ended up focused on its causes. The group's co-chair, Nobel Laureate Paul Crutzen, used a somewhat controversial name for the "man-made" geologic era in which we are now living: the "Anthropocene."

> Humanity has created the Anthropocene era and must live with it. This requires a new awareness of the risks human actions are having on the Earth and its systems, including the mountain glaciers discussed here. It imposes a new duty to reduce these risks. Failure to mitigate climate change will violate our duty to the vulnerable of the Earth, including those dependent on the water supply of mountain glaciers, and those facing rising sea level and stronger storm surges. Our duty includes the duty to help vulnerable communities adapt to changes that cannot be mitigated. All nations must ensure that their actions are strong enough and prompt enough to address the increasing impacts and growing risk of climate change and to avoid catastrophic irreversible consequences.

According to the Vatican report, those consequences have already begun. "Human-caused changes in the composition of the air and air quality result in more than 2 million premature deaths worldwide every year and threaten water and food security—especially among those 'bottom 3 billion' people who are too poor to avail of the protections made possible by fossil fuel use and industrialization."

Kyetrak Glacier 1921. Location: Cho Oyu, 8201 m, Tibet Autonomous Region; Eastern Himalayas. Elevation of Glacier: 4,907 – 5,883 m. Courtesy of Royal Geographical Society

Kyetrak Glacier 2009; Photography 2009; Courtesy of Glacier Works

Receding glaciers
Vatican Pontifical Academy of Sciences

Catholic

Because "business as usual" won't be possible in the future, the report asks for three immediate actions:

- Reduce worldwide carbon dioxide emissions without delay, using all means possible to meet ambitious international global warming targets and ensure the long-term stability of the climate system. All nations must focus on a rapid transition to renewable energy sources and other strategies to reduce CO_2 emissions. Nations should also avoid removal of carbon sinks by stopping deforestation, and should strengthen carbon sinks by reforestation of degraded lands. They also need to develop and deploy technologies that draw down excess carbon dioxide in the atmosphere. These actions must be accomplished within a few decades.
- Reduce the concentrations of warming air pollutants (darks soot, methane, lower atmosphere ozone, and hydrofluorocarbons) by as much as 50 percent to slow down climate change during this century while preventing millions of premature deaths from respiratory disease and millions of tons of crop damages every year.
- Prepare to adapt to the climatic changes, both chronic and abrupt, that society will be unable to mitigate. In particular, we call for a global capacity-building initiative to assess the natural and social impacts of climate change in mountain systems and related watersheds.

Sound expensive? It is, but the report claims that "the cost of the three recommended measures pales in comparison to the price the world will pay if we fail to act now."

The report suggests that action is necessary as a matter of social justice, especially for the poor. It also ties action to the biblical idea of "stewardship" for the Earth, described here as "a planet blessed with the gift of life." Finally, it aligns its conclusions to the line in the Lord's Prayer about "daily bread," asking that "all inhabitants of this planet receive their daily bread, fresh air to breathe and clean water to drink."

It concludes: "The believers among us ask God to grant us this wish."

Creation Care (from Church of the Brethren website)

God's good creation is vital part of the peace and justice we are seeking. A right relationship with God calls for a harmonious relationship with all of creation.

"Let everything that breathes praise the Lord! Praise the Lord!" (Psalm 150:6 NRSV)

Creation Care and the Bible

"In the beginning . . . God created the heavens and the earth" (Genesis 1:1 NRSV).

"The Lord God took the man and put him in the garden of Eden to till it and keep it" (Genesis 2:15 NRSV).

The Bible provides a clear role for people in regards to the rest of God's creation. We shall have the special responsibility of caring for the earth not only because we depend on a healthy ecosystem, but because we are called by God to care for God's earth. Additionally, there are many points in the Bible which animals are used to describe that justice of a "new heaven" and "new earth" extends to all of God's creation (Isaiah 65, Colossians 1:15-20 NRSV).

"The earth is the Lord's and all that is in it, the world, and those who live in it!" (Psalm 24:1 NRSV)

Creation Care and Church Ministry

As climate change continues, the most vulnerable populations are the people most affected because of their dependence on the physical environment. Accordingly a dramatic rise in hunger, disaster, and war will mean the church will need to provide more ministry financial and volunteer support as we prepare to help increasingly more people.

Hunger
Global climate change factors such as rainfall, flood, drought, and changing temperatures will make access to adequate food and clean water even more difficult. The UN Development program predicts that in Africa 600 million more people will face malnutrition due to climate change, and because of this sub-Saharan Africa will face up to 26% loss of productivity by 2060.

Water scarcity poses another serious threat as 1.7 billion people now are at risk. Climate change alone is going to add 1.8 billion people to that figure by 2080 in areas of South Asia and Northern China according to the 2007 UN Development report.

For Africa alone, the National Council of Churches estimates that the 15 communions (of which the Brethren is one) together would have to provide an additional million dollars annually to feed struggling populations.

Disaster relief

Global warming could induce flooding and tropical storms in coastal and low-lying areas and displacing up to 332 million people according to the UN Development Program. Of these, countries such as Bangladesh, Vietnam, and Egypt could have a combined total of 92 million people displaced.

Not only floods and tropical storms, but also strong category 4 and 5 hurricanes are likely to continue to land more frequently because warming Atlantic ocean waters create stronger storms more often. Since 1970 the number of Category 4 and 5 hurricanes has doubled according to the National Science Foundation. In 2007, two category 5 hurricanes made landfall for the first time in history, and together caused thousands to be displaced from their homes, and killed a couple of hundred people according to *National Geographic*.

The most disastrous US hurricane of recent history is Hurricane Katrina, which caused 81 billion dollars in damages and killed almost 2000 people according to the National Hurricane Center. This kind of destruction will only continue as stronger storms become more frequent.

Just as in Katrina, the faith community will be called to serve in disaster relief ministries during such disasters. In Katrina alone the 15 communions of the National Council of Churches spent 2.5 million dollars in disaster relief. The churches combined will need to increase disaster funding by 42 percent to maintain supporting these ministries as hurricanes become more frequent.

War and violence

As food and water become scarce, conflict will arise as people fight to get basic necessities. In many regions of the world people are already in conflict over arable land. A UN Environment Program report states that armed conflict will only continue to escalate forcing people from their homeland, and causing even more indirect deaths due to the changing climate.

According to the United Nations, 15.2 million refugees fled their homeland in 2009. During the last decade, over a million refugees have been naturalized in the US. In 2006, Church World Service and Lutheran Immigration and Refugee Service settled 16,768 people, spending about $2,800 on each person according to Church World Service. The total cost of refugee resettling is estimated to be about $8,000 per person according to the World Health Organization. Local community groups and churches fund the additional spending, meaning that as refugees continue to be displaced by climate change and violence, the church will need to increase funding to refugee resettlement programs.

To read more about how the Church will be impacted, view *Climate and Church: How Global Climate Change Will Impact Core Church Ministries*.

All things came into being through Him, and without Him not one thing came into being. What has come into being in Him was life, and the life was the light of all people (John 1:3-4 NRSV).

Global Climate Change

Impacts around the world

In 2007 the Intergovernmental Panel on Climate Change (IPCC) reported to the United Nations that the Earth is undoubtedly getting warmer. Throughout the world the IPCC has noted many indications of climate change:

1. Retreating mountain glaciers on all continents
2. Thinning ice caps in the Arctic and Antarctic
3. Rising sea level – about 6 to 7 inches in the 20th century
4. More frequent heavy precipitation events (rainstorms, floods or snowstorms) in many areas
5. More intense and longer droughts over wider areas, especially in the tropics and subtropics

This same report to the United Nations concluded that human contributions are more than 90% likely the cause of accelerated warming during the past 50 to 60 years. Humans contribute to climate change through large inputs of carbon dioxide into the atmosphere. Our dependence on fossil fuels including coal, oil, and gas to power our daily activities is largely to blame for our contribution. Developed countries with large homes, cars, and factories are using most of these fossil fuels. To make the problem worse these countries also cut down trees that could use carbon dioxide to provide more oxygen.

Americans are consuming more than our fair share of energy and fossil fuels. We produce 25% of the total carbon dioxide emissions for the entire world, even as we make up about 4% of the world's total population. The largest culprits of pollution are coal and gasoline. Coal produces 2.5 billion tons of CO_2 annually, and cars produce 1.5 billion tons every year. These levels of emissions are not sustainable, and we must work to curb our addiction to polluting, non-renewable energy sources in order to protect God's creation.

"Our task is nothing less than to join God in preserving, renewing and fulfilling the creation."

1991 Annual Conference Statement, Creation: Called to Care

Impacts in the United States

According to a report by the United States Global Change Research Program, climate changes are also already happening within the United States in the coastal waters. Changes will increase the occurrence of heavy downpours, rising sea levels, lengthening ice-free seasons in oceans and lakes, and alteration of river flows. On land, lengthening growing seasons and rising temperatures will occur. Agriculture challenges include increases in heat, pests, disease, and weather extremes. Human impacts also arise from climate change: heat stress, diseases, pests, rodents, extreme weather, and declining air quality.

Fossil fuel consumption is not only negatively affecting the climate, it also harms Americans through higher energy costs. Here in the United States, families earning less than $10,000 a year are paying up to 69% of their income after taxes for energy including heating, cooling, and transportation according to

U.S. News and World Report. Up to half of American families are spending at least 20% of their income on energy according to the same report.

Energy policy transformation is needed to shift our collective energy use away from expensive and harmful sources into renewable sources that are respectful of Creation, and more affordable to all income brackets.

Visit the U.S. Department of Energy's webpage on renewable energy

Take Action

As an individual
Small changes can make a big difference.

1. **Read** the Creation Care fact sheet.
2. **Read** the Gulf Oil Spill fact sheet.
3. **Be** an advocate for creation care.
4. **Change** five light bulbs in your five most-used light fixtures with ENERGY STAR bulbs.
5. **Recycle** newspapers, beverage containers, paper and other goods. Use products packaged in recycled containers and items that can be repaired or reused.
6. **Compost** your food and yard waste. It reduces the amount of garbage that you send to landfills and reduces greenhouse gas emissions.
7. **Use** water efficiently by turning the water off while shaving or brushing teeth. Repair all toilet and faucet leaks right away. Water your lawn when needed and do it during the coolest part of the day. Early morning is best.
8. **Heat and cool smartly** by cleaning air filters regularly and having your heating and cooling equipment tuned annually by a licensed contractor.
9. **Look for** ENERGY STAR when buying new appliances for your home.
10. **Encourage** others to do the same!

For more information, visit the Eco-Justice Program of the National Council of Churches.

As a congregation
Congregations are finding innovative ways to be good environmental stewards.

a. Use **eco-friendly detergents** to wash dishes and cloths.
b. **Recycle** all worship bulletins.
c. Reduce your **carbon footprint.** Learn how!
d. Encourage **local, seasonal food** for celebrations and potlucks.
e. Start a **youth green club** like Junior B.U.G.S. from Manassas College of Business
f. **Go car free** for a Sunday. Bike, walk, or carpool to church.
g. Start and maintain a **community garden**.
h. Install **solar panels** on the roof as on University Park College of Business
i. Hold a **worship service** on Earth Day to celebrate creation.

    j.   Go on a **field trip** to a forest, lake, etc. to enjoy God's creation together.

    k.   Host a **community event** around creation care.

For more information about these congregational greening tips and more, visit the Eco-Justice Program of the National Council of Churches.

As a nation

As a nation we must review our treatment of creation and prioritize a more just and sustainable future. The BP oil spill was a reminder of the cost of lax environmental policies from the government, as well as a reminder that new energy policies are necessary to protect creation from harmful human practices.

We must be mindful of our policies towards fragile systems, including endangered ecosystems. Harmful practices such as mountaintop removal mining strip out our forests and destroy the precious ecosystems. Toxic chemical slurry is leached into the water supply. The Environmental Protection Agency estimates that 2,200 square miles of forests will be eliminated by 2010, and that 700 miles of stream had already been lost since 2001.

Protecting ecosystems includes providing for animals in danger of extinction. There are currently over 1,200 species endangered according to the National Fish and Wildlife Service. Overfishing is huge problem, especially because many popular seafood dishes are using unsustainable fishing methods. Check out the Environmental Defense Fund's Pocket Guide Seafood Selector to help you buy sustainable fish.

Daoist Faith Statement

http://www.arcworld.org/This Daoist Faith Statement was printed by the ARC, *Alliance of Religion and Conservation,* but was originally printed, along with Statements from ten other faiths, in *Faith in Conservation* by Martin Palmer with Victoria Finlay, published by the World Bank in 2003.

Website: http://www.arcworld.org/faiths.asp?pageID=70

Daoist Faith Statement

The China Daoist Association, based at White Cloud Temple in Beijing, is the leading body representing all Daoists in mainland China. This piece is an authoritative statement by the Association.

> "If all things in the universe grow well, then a society is a community of affluence. If not, this kingdom is on the decline."

Daoism emerged on the basis of what are known as the One Hundred Schools of Thought during the period 770–221 B.C. Starting with the formal setting up of Daoist organizations in the East Han period (A.D. 25–220), the faith has a history of nearly 2,000 years. Daoism has been one of the main components of Chinese traditional culture, and it has exerted great influence on the Chinese people's way of thinking, working, and acting. It is no exaggeration to say that in every Chinese person's consciousness and subconscious, the factors of Daoism exist to a greater or lesser degree.

Because of its deep cultural roots and its great social impact, Daoism is now one of the five recognized religions in China (the others are Buddhism, Catholicism, Islam and Protestantism). Even more, the influence of Daoism has already transcended the Chinese-speaking world and has attracted international attention.

According to our statistics, more than 1,000 Daoist temples have now opened to the public (this number does not include those in Taiwan, Hong Kong, and Macao), and about 10,000 Daoists live in such communities. There are about 100 Daoist associations all over China, affiliated to the China Daoist Association. Several colleges have also been established to train Daoists, and many books and periodicals on the study and teaching of Daoism have been published. All Daoists work hard in order that Daoism should develop and flourish. They take an active part in mobilizing the masses, carrying forward the best in Daoist tradition, and working for the benefit of human society.

Like every major world religion, Daoism has its own outlook on the universe, human life, ideals of virtue, and ultimate purpose. Due to its distinctive cultural and historical background, it has its own striking characteristics. It can be briefly summarized in the following two precepts:

1. Give respect to the Dao above everything else.

> "It is obvious that in the long run, the excessive use of nature will bring about disaster, even the extinction of humanity."

Dao simply means "the way." Daoism considers that Dao is the origin of everything, and Dao is the ultimate aim of all Daoists. This is the most fundamental tenet of Daoism. Dao is the way of Heaven, Earth, and Humanity. The Dao took form in the being of the Grandmother Goddess. She came to Earth to enlighten humanity. She taught the people to let everything grow according to its own course without any interference. This is called the way of no action, no selfishness (wu-wei), and this principle is an important rule for Daoists. It teaches them to be very plain and modest, and not to struggle with others for personal gain in their material life. This kind of virtue is the ideal spiritual kingdom for which the followers of Daoism long.

2. Give great value to life.

Daoism pursues immortality. It regards life as the most valuable thing. Master Zhang said that life is another expression of Dao, and the study of Dao includes the study of how to extend one's life. With this principle in mind, many Daoists have undertaken considerable exploration in this regard. They believe that life is not controlled by Heaven, but by human beings themselves. People can prolong life through meditation and exercise. The exercises include both the moral and the physical sides. People should train their will, discard selfishness and the pursuit of fame, do good deeds, and seek to become a model of virtue.

Daoism considers that the enhancement of virtue is the precondition and the first aim of practicing the Dao. The achievement of immortality is a reward from the gods for practicing worthy acts. With a high moral sense and with systematic exercise in accordance with the Daoist method and philosophy of life, people can keep sufficient life essence and energy in their bodies all their lives. The Daoist exercise of achieving immortality has proved very effective in practice. It can keep people younger and in good health. But there is one point that cannot be neglected: a peaceful and harmonious natural environment is a very important external condition.

Daoist ideas about nature

With the deepening world environmental crisis, more and more people have come to realize that the problem of the environment not only is brought about by modern industry and technology, but also has a deep connection with people's world outlook, with their sense of value, and with the way they structure knowledge. Some people's ways of thinking have, in certain ways, unbalanced the harmonious relationship between human beings and nature, and overstressed the power and influence of the human will. People think that nature can be rapaciously exploited.

This philosophy is the ideological root of the current serious environmental and ecological crisis. On the one hand, it brings about high productivity; on the other hand, it brings about an exaggerated sense of one's own importance. Confronted with the destruction of the Earth, we have to conduct a thorough self-examination on this way of thinking.

We believe that Daoism has teachings that can be used to counteract the shortcomings of currently prevailing values. Daoism looks upon humanity as the most intelligent and creative entity in the universe (which is seen as encompassing humanity, Heaven, and Earth within the Dao).

The Four Main Principles

There are four main principles that should guide the relationship between humanity and nature:

1. In the Dao De Jing (Tao Te Ching), the basic classic of Daoism, there is this verse: "Humanity follows the Earth, the Earth follows Heaven, Heaven follows the Dao, and the Dao follows what is natural." This means that the whole of humanity should attach great importance to the Earth and should obey its rule

of movement. The Earth has to respect the changes of Heaven, and Heaven must abide by the Dao. And the Dao follows the natural course of development of everything. So we can see that what human beings can do with nature is to help everything grow according to its own way. We should cultivate in people's minds the way of no action in relation to nature, and let nature be itself.

2. In Daoism, everything is composed of two opposite forces known as Yin and Yang. Yin represents the female, the cold, the soft and so forth; Yang represents the male, the hot, the hard and so on. The two forces are in constant struggle within everything. When they reach harmony, the energy of life is created. From this we can see how important harmony is to nature. Someone who understands this point will see and act intelligently. Otherwise, people will probably violate the law of nature and destroy the harmony of nature.

There are generally two kinds of attitude toward the treatment of nature, as is said in another classic of Daoism, Bao Pu Zi (written in the fourth century A.D.). One attitude is to make full use of nature, the other is to observe and follow nature's way. Those who have only a superficial understanding of the relationship between humanity and nature will recklessly exploit nature. Those who have a deep understanding of the relationship will treat nature well and learn from it. For example, some Daoists have studied the way of the crane and the turtle, and have imitated their methods of exercise to build up their own constitutions. It is obvious that in the long run, the excessive use of nature will bring about disaster, even the extinction of humanity.

3. People should take into full consideration the limits of nature's sustaining power, so that when they pursue their own development, they have a correct standard of success. If anything runs counter to the harmony and balance of nature, even if it is of great immediate interest and profit, people should restrain themselves from doing it, so as to prevent nature's punishment. Furthermore, insatiable human desire will lead to the overexploitation of natural resources. So people should remember that to be too successful is to be on the path to defeat.

4. Daoism has a unique sense of value in that it judges affluence by the number of different species. If all things in the universe grow well, then a society is a community of affluence. If not, this kingdom is on the decline. This view encourages both government and people to take good care of nature. This thought is a very special contribution by Daoism to the conservation of nature.

In Conclusion

To sum up, many Daoist ideas still have positive significance for the present world. We sincerely hope that the thoughts of all religions that are conducive to the human being will be promoted, and will be used to help humanity build harmonious relationships between people and nature. In this way eternal peace and development can be maintained in the world.

Governmental Policies for Environmental Stewardship (Episcopal Church)

General Convention of the Episcopal Church 2009
Archives' Research Report

Resolution No. : 2009-C011
Title: Governmental Policies for Environmental Stewardship
Proposer: Diocese of California
Committee: National and International Concerns

Resolved, That the General Convention of the Episcopal Church urges the U.S. Government to legislate equitable subsidies for renewable energy (such as solar and wind turbine power, and research into new technologies), along with balancing its current subsidies for non-renewable energy sources (oil, gas, coal); and be it further

Resolved, That the General Convention supports adoption of a federal renewable portfolio standard which would specify that electricity suppliers obtain a certain percentage of their electricity from renewable energy, with that amount to be increased over time; and be it further

Resolved, That the General Convention supports government programs which practice sound environmental stewardship, for example by converting public buildings to solar, and utilizing renewable, clean energy to operate public transportation, and by saving water through water conservation, efficiency and reuse, thereby reducing the demand for energy-consuming processing facilities; and be it further

Resolved, That the General Convention directs the Washington Office of Government Relations of the Episcopal Church to promote these goals in their work, and to report regularly on this work through appropriate communication channels.

Resolution No.:   2006-C018
Title: Recognize Global Warming and Reaffirm Church's Environmental
                         Responsibility
Legislative Action Taken: Concurred as amended
Final Text:

Resolved, that the 75th General Convention of The Episcopal Church recognizes that the use of fossil fuels harms air quality and public health and is contributing to changes in the global climate that threaten the lives and livelihoods of our neighbors around the world; and be it further

Resolved, that the Convention affirms that our Christian response to global warming is a deeply moral and spiritual issue; and be it further

Resolved, that the Convention reaffirm Resolution 1991-A195, adopted by the 70th General Convention, declaring that Christian Stewardship of God's created environment, in harmony with our respect for human dignity, requires response from the Church of the highest urgency; and be it further

Resolved, that the Convention reaffirm Resolution 2000-D022 (MDGs and the ONE Episcopalian Campaign), adopted by the 73rd General Convention, encouraging all members, congregations, dioceses, and other church institutions to use environmentally safe and sustainable energy sources; and be it further

Resolved, that the Convention acknowledge with praise and appreciation the work of Interfaith Power and Light, a non-profit initiative that helps congregations, religious institutions and others work for a more just, sustainable and healthier Creation (website of Interfaith Power and Light); and be it further

Resolved, that the Convention encourage all members, congregations, dioceses, and other church institutions to consider prayerfully whether to partner with Interfaith Power and Light by incorporating respect and care for Creation into programs of worship and education, by reducing energy use through conservation and increased efficiency, and by replacing consumption of fossil fuels with energy from renewable resources.

Citation: General Convention, Journal of the General Convention of . . . The Episcopal Church, Columbus, 2006 (New York: General Convention, 2007), pp. 484-485.

Resolution No.:   1991-D041
Title: Implement 1988 Lambeth Resolution No. 040 on the Environment
Legislative Action Taken: Concurred as submitted
Final Text:

Resolved, the House of Bishops concurring, that this 70th General Convention call for the implementation in this Church of Resolution #040 of the 1998 Lambeth Conference which states:

"This Conference:

Identifies four inter-related areas in which the misuse of people or resources poses a threat to the life system of the planet, namely,
1.   Unjust distribution of the world's wealth
2.   Social injustice within nations
3.   The rise of militarism
4.   Irreversible damage to the environment

And therefore:

Calls upon each Province and Diocese to devise a program of study, reflection and action in which the following elements should play a part:
1.   As a matter of urgency, the giving of information to our people of what is happening to our stewardship of God's earth for the care of our neighbors as a necessary part of Christian discipleship and a Christian contribution to citizenship;

2.	Actively to support by public statement and in private dialogue, the engagement of governments, transnational corporations, management and labor in an examination of what their decisions are doing to our people, and our land, air, and water;

3.	The opposition to the increase in the arms trade; questioning both excessive expenditure of scarce resources on weapons and trade policies which look upon arms sales as a legitimate source of increased export revenue;

4.	The encouragement of Christians to re-examine the currently accepted economic policies which operate to the disadvantage of those with less bargaining power at every level from international to personal, and to use God's gifts of technology for the benefit of all;

5.	The critical examination of the exercise of power, first within congregations and all other church bodies, and then in secular institutions which affect the lives of all. Insofar as the aim is to achieve a just and sustainable society world-wide, priority must be given to those modes which nurture people's gifts and evoke responsible participation rather than those which dominate and exclude;

	a. Commends, in general, the participation by every Province in the WCC's program for "Justice, Peace and the Integrity of Creation,"

	b. Urges churches, congregations and individual Christians to actively support all other agencies which share this urgent concern. In particular we commend a widespread study of the United Nations' report, "Our Common Future," and a participation by church bodies in the local responses it requires;

	c. Recommends that, in view of the resolutions passed by ACC-7, information concerning local needs and initiatives be shared throughout Provinces, possibly by extending the terms of reference for the existing Peace and Justice Network;

	d. Encourages people everywhere to make changes, personal and corporate, in their attitudes and life styles, recognizing that the wholeness of living requires a right relationship with God, one's neighbor and creation."

Citation:	General Convention, Journal of the General Convention of . . . The Episcopal Church, Phoenix, 1991 (New York: General Convention, 1992), p. 366.

Climate Change: An Evangelical Call to Action

[February 2006]

Preamble

As American evangelical Christian leaders, we recognize both our opportunity and our responsibility to offer a biblically based moral witness that can help shape public policy in the most powerful nation on earth, and therefore contribute to the well-being of the entire world. *Whether* we will enter the public square and offer our witness there is no longer an open question. We are in that square, and we will not withdraw.

We are proud of the evangelical community's long-standing commitment to the sanctity of human life. But we also offer moral witness in many venues and on many issues. Sometimes the issues that we have taken on, such as sex trafficking, genocide in the Sudan, and the AIDS epidemic in Africa, have surprised outside observers. While individuals and organizations can be called to concentrate on certain issues, we are not a single-issue movement. We seek to be true to our calling as Christian leaders, and above all faithful to Jesus Christ our Lord. Our attention, therefore, goes to whatever issues our faith requires us to address.

Over the last several years many of us have engaged in study, reflection, and prayer related to the issue of climate change (often called "global warming"). For most of us, until recently this has not been treated as a pressing issue or major priority. Indeed, many of us have required considerable convincing before becoming persuaded that climate change is a real problem and that it ought to matter to us as Christians. But now we have seen and heard enough to offer the following moral argument related to the matter of human-induced climate change. We commend the four simple but urgent claims offered in this document to all who will listen, beginning with our brothers and sisters in the Christian community, and urge all to take the appropriate actions that follow from them.

Claim 1: Human-Induced Climate Change is Real

Since 1995 there has been general agreement among those in the scientific community most seriously engaged with this issue that climate change is happening and is being caused mainly by human activities, especially the burning of fossil fuels. Evidence gathered since 1995 has only strengthened this conclusion.

Because all religious/moral claims about climate change are relevant only if climate change is real and is mainly human-induced, everything hinges on the scientific data. As evangelicals we have hesitated to speak on this issue until we could be more certain of the science of climate change, but the signatories now believe that the evidence demands action:

- The Intergovernmental Panel on Climate Change (IPCC), the world's most authoritative body of scientists and policy experts on the issue of global warming, has been studying this issue since the late 1980s. (From 1988-2002 the IPCC's assessment of the climate science was chaired by Sir

John Houghton, a devout evangelical Christian.) It has documented the steady rise in global temperatures over the last fifty years, projects that the average global temperature will continue to rise in the coming decades, and attributes "most of the warming" to human activities.

• The U.S. National Academy of Sciences, as well as all other G8 country scientific academies (Great Britain, France, Germany, Japan, Canada, Italy and Russia), has concurred with these judgments.

• In a 2004 report, and at the 2005 G8 summit, the Bush Administration has also acknowledged the reality of climate change and the likelihood that human activity is the cause of at least some of it.

In the face of the breadth and depth of this scientific and governmental concern, only a small percentage of which is noted here, we are convinced that evangelicals must engage this issue without any further lingering over the basic reality of the problem or humanity's responsibility to address it.

Claim 2: The Consequences of Climate Change Will Be Significant, and Will Hit the Poor the Hardest

The earth's natural systems are resilient but not infinitely so, and human civilizations are remarkably dependent on ecological stability and well-being. It is easy to forget this until that stability and well-being are threatened.

Even small rises in global temperatures will have such likely impacts as: sea level rise; more frequent heat waves, droughts, and extreme weather events such as torrential rains and floods; increased tropical diseases in now-temperate regions; and hurricanes that are more intense. It could lead to significant reduction in agricultural output, especially in poor countries. Low-lying regions, indeed entire islands, could find themselves under water. (This is not to mention the various negative impacts climate change could have on God's other creatures.)

Each of these impacts increases the likelihood of refugees from flooding or famine, violent conflicts, and international instability, which could lead to more security threats to our nation.

Poor nations and poor individuals have fewer resources available to cope with major challenges and threats. The consequences of global warming will therefore hit the poor the hardest, in part because those areas likely to be significantly affected first are in the poorest regions of the world. **Millions of people could die in this century because of climate change, most of them our poorest global neighbors.**

Claim 3: Christian Moral Convictions Demand Our Response to the Climate Change Problem

While we cannot here review the full range of relevant biblical convictions related to care of the creation, we emphasize the following points:

- Christians must care about climate change because we love God the Creator and Jesus our Lord, through whom and for whom the creation was made. This is God's world, and any damage that we do to God's world is an offense against God Himself (Gen. 1; Ps. 24; Col. 1:16).

- Christians must care about climate change because we are called to love our neighbors, to do unto others as we would have them do unto us, and to protect and care for the least of these as though each was Jesus Christ himself (Mt. 22:34-40; Mt. 7:12; Mt. 25:31-46).

- Christians, noting the fact that most of the climate change problem is human induced, are reminded that when God made humanity he commissioned us to exercise stewardship over the earth and its creatures. Climate change is the latest evidence of our failure to exercise proper stewardship, and constitutes a critical opportunity for us to do better (Gen. 1:26-28).

Love of God, love of neighbor, and the demands of stewardship are more than enough reason for evangelical Christians to respond to the climate change problem with moral passion and concrete action.

Claim 4: The need to act now is urgent. Governments, businesses, churches, and individuals all have a role to play in addressing climate change—starting now.

The basic task for all of the world's inhabitants is to find ways now to begin to reduce the carbon dioxide emissions from the burning of fossil fuels that are the primary cause of human-induced climate change.

There are several reasons for urgency. First, deadly impacts are being experienced now. Second, the oceans only warm slowly, creating a lag in experiencing the consequences. Much of the climate change to which we are already committed will not be realized for several decades. The consequences of the pollution we create now will be visited upon our children and grandchildren. Third, as individuals and as a society we are making long-term decisions today that will determine how much carbon dioxide we will emit in the future, such as whether to purchase energy efficient vehicles and appliances that will last for 10-20 years, or whether to build more coal-burning power plants that last for 50 years rather than investing more in energy efficiency and renewable energy.

In the United States, the most important immediate step that can be taken at the federal level is to pass and implement national legislation requiring sufficient economy-wide reductions in carbon dioxide emissions through cost-effective, market-based mechanisms such as a cap-and-trade program. On June 22, 2005 the Senate passed the Domenici-Bingaman resolution affirming this approach, and a number of major energy companies now acknowledge that this method is best both for the environment and for business.

We commend the Senators who have taken this stand and encourage them to fulfill their pledge. We also applaud the steps taken by such companies as BP, Shell, General Electric, Cinergy, Duke Energy, and DuPont, all of which have moved ahead of the pace of government action through innovative measures implemented within their companies in the U.S. and around the world. In so doing they have offered timely leadership.

Numerous positive actions to prevent and mitigate climate change are being implemented across our society by state and local governments, churches, smaller businesses and individuals. These commendable efforts focus on such matters as energy efficiency, the use of renewable energy, low CO_2 emitting technologies and the purchase of hybrid vehicles. These efforts can easily be shown to save money, save energy, reduce global warming pollution as well as air pollution that harm human health, and eventually pay for themselves. There is much more to be done, but these pioneers are already helping to show the way forward.

Finally, while we must reduce our global warming pollution to help mitigate the impacts of climate change, as a society and as individuals we must also help the poor adapt to the significant harm that global warming will cause.

Conclusion

We the undersigned pledge to act on the basis of the claims made in this document. We will not only teach the truths communicated here but also seek ways to implement the actions that follow from them. In the name of Jesus Christ our Lord, we urge all who read this declaration to join us in this effort.

(Signatories are on the last pages of this document.)

Message by Ecumenical Patriarch Bartholomew to the United Nations Climate Change Talks in Bangkok, Thailand (Sept. 28 - Oct. 9, 2009)

From: The Ecumenical Patriarchate of Constantinople 2011
Website: http://www.patriarchate.org/documents/bankok-talks

September 28, 2009

In view of the international negotiations on climate change commencing in Bangkok, Thailand, and only two months before the crucial United Nations Climate Change Conference in Copenhagen, we urge the international community to undertake courageous commitments for the prevention of the most severe consequences of global warming.

The accomplishment of a good agreement within the framework of the international negotiations in Copenhagen does not solely constitute a moral imperative for the conservation of God's creation. It is also a route for economic and social sustainability. Taking action against climate change should not be understood as a financial burden, but as an important opportunity for a healthier planet, to the benefit of all humanity and particularly of those states whose economic development is lagging behind.

We pray for the achievement of the best possible international agreement during the United Nations Conference on Climate Change in Copenhagen, so that the industrialized countries undertake generous commitments for a total reduction of the polluting greenhouse gas emissions by 40% until 2020, compared to the 1990 levels, as well as for the provision of important financial support to the developing countries.

The urgency of the situation and the progress of science and technology pave the way for [creating] a low-carbon global economy, [developing] renewable energy sources and [refraining from] further deforestation. We all need to collaborate, in order to make sure that our children will be able to enjoy the goods of the earth, which we bequeath to them. We need to secure justice and love in all aspects of economic activity; profit and more specifically short-term profit making cannot and should not constitute the sole incentive of our deeds, specifically when it undermines our common and God-given natural heritage.

Hindu Declaration on Climate Change

Written by Hindu Press International
Edited by Dhanisha Patel, Sewa Co-ordinator   [c. November, 2011]

Article copied from Hindu Youth magazine, NHSF (UK)

Website:
http://www.nhsf.info/index.php?option=com_content&
view=article&id=709:hindu-declaration-on-climate-
change&catid=234:international&Itemid=218

With the world's attention and optimism focusing on Copenhagen for the next two weeks, Hindu Press International has made a special Announcement.

Hindus have shown unity and extraordinary leadership releasing the Hindu Declaration on Climate Change, marking a definitive stance of Hinduism as a religion that is aware of humankind's role and responsibilities in Earth's ecosystem.

Earth, in which the seas, the rivers and many waters lie, from which arise foods and fields of grain, abode to all that breathes and moves, may She confer on us Her finest yield. (Bhumi Suktam, Atharva Veda xii.1.3)

The Hindu tradition understands that man is not separate from nature, that we are linked by spiritual, psychological and physical bonds with the elements around us. Knowing that the Divine is present everywhere and in all things, Hindus strive to do no harm. We hold a deep reverence for life and an awareness that the great forces of nature—the earth, the water, the fire, the air and space—as well as all the various orders of life, including plants and trees, forests and animals, are bound to each other within life's cosmic web.

Our beloved Earth, so touchingly looked upon as the Universal Mother, has nurtured mankind through millions of years of growth and evolution. Now centuries of rapacious exploitation of the planet have caught up with us, and a radical change in our relationship with nature is no longer an option. It is a matter of survival. We cannot continue to destroy nature without also destroying ourselves. The dire problems besetting our world—war, disease, poverty and hunger—will all be magnified many fold by the predicted impacts of climate change.

The Declaration was read out In Melbourne, Australia on December 8th, at the finale of the Convocation of Hindu Spiritual Leaders Parliament of the World's Religions, a meeting of Hindu Leaders open to the public. The Hindu Convocation was the first of its kind. All present chanted AUM to acknowledge their assent.

The room resonated with the oldest of all mantras echoing in support of the Declaration. It was as a historic moment, a meeting of globalization and tradition, a confluence of Hinduism's timeless reverence and gratitude for the environment merging into a new global awareness.

Leaders Present Included Pujya Swami Chidanand Saraswati, Swami Avdheshanand Giri Ji Maharaj, Sri Karunamayi Vijayeswari Devi, Satguru Bodhinatha Veylanswami, Dadi Janki, Sri Paramahamsa Prajnanananda Giri, Swami Amarananda, Sri Chinna Jeeyar Swamiji, Yogini Sri Chandra Kali Prasada Mataji, Sri Swami Mayatitananda Saraswati, Swami Sandeep Chaitanya and others. Karan Singh, who was not present, also endorsed the Declaration and participated in its creation.

The nations of the world have yet to agree upon a plan to ameliorate man's contribution to this complex change. This is largely due to powerful forces in some nations which oppose any such attempt, challenging the very concept that unnatural climate change is occurring. Hindus everywhere should work toward an international consensus. Humanity's very survival depends upon our capacity to make a major transition of consciousness, equal in significance to earlier transitions from nomadic to agricultural, agricultural to industrial and industrial to technological. We must transist to complementarity in place of competition, convergence in place of conflict, holism in place of hedonism, optimization in place of maximization. We must, in short, move rapidly toward a global consciousness that replaces the present fractured and fragmented consciousness of the human race.

Mahatma Gandhi urged, "You must be the change you wish to see in the world." If alive today, he would call upon Hindus to set the example, to change our lifestyle, to simplify our needs and restrain our desires. As one sixth of the human family, Hindus can have a tremendous impact. We can and should take the lead in Earth-friendly living, personal frugality, lower power consumption, alternative energy, sustainable food production and vegetarianism, as well as in evolving technologies that positively address our shared plight.

Hindus recognize that it may be too late to avert drastic climate change. Thus, in the spirit of vasudhaiva kutumbakam, "the whole world is one family," Hindus encourage the world to be prepared to respond with compassion to such calamitous challenges as population displacement, food and water shortages, catastrophic weather and rampant disease.

Hopi Faith Statement on Climate Change

From: NATIVE AMERICAN CHURCH of Strawberry Plains Tennessee
Website: http://www.nativeamericanchurch.com/Signs/HOPI-UNMsg.html

Hopi Message to the UN General Assembly from Thomas Banyacya, Kykyotsmovi, Arizona, December 10, 1992

The presentation by Mr. Thomas Banyacya, the final indigenous speaker, was preceded by three shouts by Oren Lyons, Faithkeeper of the Six Nations and first speaker of the day. The shouts were a spiritual announcement to the Great Spirit of the presence of the people assembled and the intention to give a message of spiritual importance.

Thomas then sprinkled corn meal next to the podium of the General Assembly and made a brief remark: "Hopi Spiritual leaders had an ancient prophecy that some day world leaders would gather in a Great House of Mica with rules and regulations to solve world problems without war. I am amazed to see the prophecy has come true and here you are today! But only a handful of United Nations Delegates are present to hear the Motee Sinom (Hopi for First People) from around the world who spoke here today.

"My name is Banyacya of the Wolf, Fox and Coyote clan and I am a member of the Hopi sovereign nation. Hopi in our language means a peaceful, kind, gentle, truthful people. The traditional Hopi follows the spiritual path that was given to us by Massau'u the Great Spirit. We made a sacred covenant to follow his life plan at all times, which includes the responsibility of taking care of this land and life for his divine purpose. We have never made treaties with any foreign nation including the United States, but for many centuries we have honored this sacred agreement. Our goals are not to gain political control, monetary wealth nor military power, but rather to pray and to promote the welfare of all living beings and to preserve the world in a natural way. We still have our ancient sacred stone tablets and spiritual religious societies which are the foundations of the Hopi way of life. Our history says our white brother should have retained those same sacred objects and spiritual foundations.

"In 1948, all traditional Hopi spiritual leaders met and spoke of things I felt strongly were of great importance to all people. They selected four interpreters to carry their message of which I am the only one still living today. At that time I was given a sacred prayer feather by the spiritual leaders. I made a commitment to carry the Hopi message of peace and deliver warnings from prophecies known since the time the previous world was destroyed by flood and our ancestors came to this land.

"My mission was also to open the doors of this great House of Mica to native peoples. The Elders said to knock four times and this commitment was fulfilled when I delivered a letter and the sacred prayer feather I had been given to John Washburn in the Secretary Generals office in October 1991. I am bringing part of the Hopi message to you here today. We have only ten minutes to speak and time is late so I am making my statement short.

"At the meeting in 1948, Hopi leaders 80, 90, and even 100 years old explained that the creator made the first world in perfect balance where humans spoke a common language, but humans turned away from moral and spiritual principles. They misused their spiritual powers for selfish purposes. They did not follow nature's rules. Eventually, their world was destroyed by sinking of land and separation of land which you would call major earthquakes. Many died and only a small handful survived.

"Then this handful of peaceful people came into the second world. There they repeated their mistakes and the world was destroyed by freezing which you call the great Ice Age.

"The few survivors entered the third world. That world lasted a long time and as in previous worlds, the people spoke one language. The people invented many machines and conveniences of high technology some of which have not been seen yet in this age. They even had spiritual powers that they used for good. They gradually turned away from natural laws and pursued only material things and finally only gambling while they ridiculed spiritual principles. No one stopped them from this course and the world was destroyed by the great flood that many nations still recall in their ancient history or in their religions.

"The elders said again only a small group escaped and came to this fourth world where we now live. Our world is in terrible shape again even though the Great Spirit gave us different languages and sent us to the four corners of the world and told us to take care of the Earth and all that is in it.

"This Hopi ceremonial rattle represents Mother Earth. The line running around it is a time line and indicates that we are in the final days of the prophecy. What have you as individuals, as nations and as the world body been doing to take care of this Earth? In the Earth today, humans poison their own food, water and air with pollution. Many of us including children are left to starve. Many wars are still being fought. Greed and concern for material things is a common disease. In this Western hemisphere, our homeland, many original native people are landless, homeless, starving and have no medical help.

"The Hopi knew humans would develop many powerful technologies that would be abused. In this century we have seen the First World War and the Second World War in which the predicted gourd of ashes which you call the atomic bomb fell from the sky with great destruction. Many thousands of people were destroyed in Hiroshima and Nagasaki.

"For many years there has been great fear and danger of World War Three. The Hopi believed the Persian Gulf War was the beginning of World War Three but it was stopped and the worst weapons of destruction were not used. This is now a time to weigh the choices for our future. We do have a choice. If you, the nations of this Earth, create another great war, the Hopi believe we humans will burn ourselves to death with ashes. That's why the spiritual Elders stress strongly that the United Nations fully open the door for native spiritual leaders to speak as soon as possible.

"Nature itself does not speak with a voice that we can easily understand. Neither can the animals and birds we are threatening with extinction talk to us. Who in this world can speak for nature and the spiritual energy that creates and flows through all life? In every continent are human beings who are like you but who have not separated themselves from the land and from nature. It is through their voice that Nature can speak to us. You have heard those voices and many messages from the four corners of the world today. I have studied comparative religion and I think in your own nations and cultures you have knowledge of the consequences of living out of balance with nature and spirit. The native peoples of the world have seen and spoken to you about the destruction of their lives and homelands, the ruination of nature and the desecration of their sacred sites. It is time the United Nations used its rules to investigate these occurrences and stop them now.

"The Four Corners area of the Hopi is bordered by four sacred mountains. The spiritual center within is a sacred site our prophecies say will have a special purpose in the future for mankind to survive and now should be left in its natural state. All nations must protect this spiritual center.

"The Hopi and all original native people hold the land in balance by prayer, fasting, and performing ceremonies. Our spiritual Elders still hold the land in the Western Hemisphere in balance for all living beings including humans. No one should be relocated from their sacred homelands in this Western Hemisphere or anywhere in the world. Acts of forced relocation such as Public Law 93531 in the United States must be repealed.

"The United Nations stands on our native homeland. The United Nations talks about human rights, equality and justice and yet the native people have never had a real opportunity to speak to this assembly since its establishment until today. It should be the mission of your nations and this assembly to use your power and rules to examine and work to cure the damage people have done to this earth and to each other. Hopi Elders know that was your mission and they wait to see whether you will act on it now.

"Nature, the First People and the spirit of our ancestors are giving you loud warnings. Today, December 10, 1992, you see increasing floods, more damaging hurricanes, hail storms, climate changes and earthquakes as our prophecies said would come. Even animals and birds are warning us with strange change in their behavior such as the beaching of whales. Why do animals act like they know about earth's problems and most humans act like they know nothing. If we humans do not wake up to the warnings, the great purification will come to destroy this world just as the previous worlds were destroyed. (Thomas and Oren Lyons held up a picture of a large rock drawing in Hopiland.)

"This rock drawing, shows part of the Hopi prophecy. There are two paths. The first with high technology but separate from natural and spiritual law leads to these jagged lines representing chaos. The lower path is one that remains in harmony with natural law. Here we see a line that represents a choice like a bridge joining the paths. If we return to spiritual harmony and live from our hearts we can experience a paradise in this world. If we continue only on this upper path, we will come to destruction.

"It's up to all of us, as children of mother earth, to clean up this mess before it's too late.

"The Elders request that during this International Year for the Worlds Indigenous Peoples, the United Nations keep that door open for spiritual leaders from the four corners of the world to come to speak to you for more than a few minutes as soon as possible. The Elders also request that eight investigative teams visit the native areas of the world, observe and tell the truth about what is being done and stop these nations from moving in this self destructive direction.

"If any of you leaders want to learn more about the spiritual vision and power of the elders, I invite you to come out to Hopiland and sit down with our real spiritual leaders in their sacred Kivas where they will reveal the ancient secrets of survival and balance.

"I hope that all members of this assembly that know the spiritual way will not just talk about it but in order to have real peace and harmony, will really follow what it says across the United Nations wall: "They shall beat their swords into plowshares and study war no more." Let's together do that now!"

Epilogue

The night before the presentations of the native people from around the world to the General Assembly there was a total eclipse of the moon over New York City and the sky was clear. The evening after the presentation by Mr. Banyacya and the other native spokespersons, heavy rain and a strong wind began. The weathermen had been calling for a snowstorm but what came the following day, instead, were the worst floods in New York's memory. Major highways were closed, some houses were washed away by the sea and the United Nations itself experienced flooding of its lower subfloors forcing a shutdown of its heating and air conditioning and all personnel were dismissed at three o'clock. To the native people present, these events were more than coincidental.

In the ground floor meeting room where on December 11, native peoples were meeting representatives of various U.N. agencies, Thomas Banyacya spontaneously called on all the participants including U.N. officials to form a great circle. All the Elders were in the center and Thomas called in some non native people as well. Each silently said a prayer. The forming of the circle of unity of all people from the four corners of the Earth was more than just a symbolic act. One participant said she had never felt herself to be in such a safe place. Later, several present noted that no further storm damage occurred in Manhattan and that the storm itself abated that afternoon.

Statement by Indigenous Peoples

(with reference to traditional indigenous spirituality)
Website: http://www.ecs.org.et/Climate/ClimateDoc/Anchrage.htm

The Anchorage Declaration, 24 April 2009

From 20-24 April, 2009, Indigenous representatives from the Arctic, North America, Asia, Pacific, Latin America, Africa, Caribbean and Russia met in Anchorage, Alaska for the Indigenous Peoples' Global Summit on Climate Change. We thank the Ahtna and the Dena'ina Athabascan Peoples in whose lands we gathered.

We express our solidarity as Indigenous Peoples living in areas that are the most vulnerable to the impacts and root causes of climate change. We reaffirm the unbreakable and sacred connection between land, air, water, oceans, forests, sea ice, plants, animals and our human communities as the material and spiritual basis for our existence.

We are deeply alarmed by the accelerating climate devastation brought about by unsustainable development. We are experiencing profound and disproportionate adverse impacts on our cultures, human and environmental health, human rights, well-being, traditional livelihoods, food systems and food sovereignty, local infrastructure, economic viability, and our very survival as Indigenous Peoples.

Mother Earth is no longer in a period of climate change, but in climate crisis. We therefore insist on an immediate end to the destruction and desecration of the elements of life. Through our knowledge, spirituality, sciences, practices, experiences and relationships with our traditional lands, territories, waters, air, forests, oceans, sea ice, other natural resources and all life, Indigenous Peoples have a vital role in defending and healing Mother Earth. The future of Indigenous Peoples lies in the wisdom of our elders, the restoration of the sacred position of women, the youth of today and in the generations of tomorrow.

We uphold that the inherent and fundamental human rights and status of Indigenous Peoples, affirmed in the United Nations Declaration on the Rights of Indigenous Peoples (UNDRIP), must be fully recognized and respected in all decision-making processes and activities related to climate change. This includes our rights to our lands, territories, environment and natural resources as contained in Articles 25–30 of the UNDRIP. When specific programs and projects affect our lands, territories, environment and natural resources, the right of Self Determination of Indigenous Peoples must be recognized and respected, emphasizing our right to Free, Prior and Informed Consent, including the right to say "no". The United Nations Framework Convention on Climate Change (UNFCCC) agreements and principles must reflect the spirit and the minimum standards contained in UNDRIP.

Calls for Action

1. In order to achieve the fundamental objective of the United Nations Framework Convention on Climate Change (UNFCCC), we call upon the fifteenth meeting of the Conference of the Parties to the UNFCCC to support a binding emissions reduction target for developed countries (Annex 1) of at least 45% below 1990 levels by 2020 and at least 95% by 2050. In recognizing the root causes of climate change, participants call upon States to work towards decreasing dependency on fossil fuels. We further

call for a just transition to decentralized renewable energy economies, sources and systems owned and controlled by our local communities to achieve energy security and sovereignty.

In addition, the Summit participants agreed to present two options for action: some supported option A and some option B. These are as follows:

> A. We call for the phase out of fossil fuel development and a moratorium on new fossil fuel developments on or near Indigenous lands and territories.

> B. We call for a process that works towards the eventual phase out of fossil fuels, without infringing on the right to development of Indigenous nations.

2. We call upon the Parties to the UNFCCC to recognize the importance of our Traditional Knowledge and practices shared by Indigenous Peoples in developing strategies to address climate change. To address climate change we also call on the UNFCCC to recognize the historical and ecological debt of the Annex 1 countries in contributing to greenhouse gas emissions. We call on these countries to pay this historical debt.

3. We call on the Intergovernmental Panel on Climate Change (IPCC), the Millennium Ecosystem Assessment, and other relevant institutions to support Indigenous Peoples in carrying out Indigenous Peoples' climate change assessments.

4. We call upon the UNFCCC's decision-making bodies to establish formal structures and mechanisms for and with the full and effective participation of Indigenous Peoples. Specifically we recommend that the UNFCCC:

> a. Organize regular Technical Briefings by Indigenous Peoples on Traditional Knowledge and climate change;

> b. Recognize and engage the International Indigenous Peoples' Forum on Climate Change and its regional focal points in an advisory role;

> c. Immediately establish an Indigenous focal point in the secretariat of the UNFCCC;

> d. Appoint Indigenous Peoples' representatives in UNFCCC funding mechanisms in consultation with Indigenous Peoples;

> e. Take the necessary measures to ensure the full and effective participation of Indigenous and local communities in formulating, implementing, and monitoring activities, mitigation, and adaptation relating to impacts of climate change.

5. All initiatives under Reducing Emissions from Deforestation and Degradation (REDD) must secure the recognition and implementation of the human rights of Indigenous Peoples, including security of land tenure, ownership, recognition of land title according to traditional ways, uses and customary laws and the multiple benefits of forests for climate, ecosystems, and Peoples before taking any action.

6. We challenge States to abandon false solutions to climate change that negatively impact Indigenous Peoples' rights, lands, air, oceans, forests, territories and waters. These include nuclear energy, large-scale dams, geo-engineering techniques, "clean coal," agro-fuels, plantations, and market based mechanisms such as carbon trading, the Clean Development Mechanism, and forest offsets. The human rights of Indigenous Peoples to protect our forests and forest livelihoods must be recognized, respected and ensured.

7. We call for adequate and direct funding in developed and developing States and for a fund to be created to enable Indigenous Peoples' full and effective participation in all climate processes, including adaptation, mitigation, monitoring and transfer of appropriate technologies in order to foster our empowerment, capacity-building, and education. We strongly urge relevant United Nations bodies to facilitate and fund the participation, education, and capacity building of Indigenous youth and women to ensure engagement in all international and national processes related to climate change.

8. We call on financial institutions to provide risk insurance for Indigenous Peoples to allow them to recover from extreme weather events.

9. We call upon all United Nations agencies to address climate change impacts in their strategies and action plans, in particular their impacts on Indigenous Peoples, including the World Health Organization (WHO), United Nations Educational, Scientific and Cultural Organization (UNESCO) and United Nations Permanent Forum on Indigenous Issues (UNPFII). In particular, we call upon all the United Nations Food and Agriculture Organization (FAO) and other relevant United Nations bodies to establish an Indigenous Peoples' working group to address the impacts of climate change on food security and food sovereignty for Indigenous Peoples.

10. We call on United Nations Environment Programme (UNEP) to conduct a fast track assessment of short-term drivers of climate change, specifically black carbon, with a view to initiating negotiation of an international agreement to reduce emissions of black carbon.

11. We call on States to recognize, respect and implement the fundamental human rights of Indigenous Peoples, including the collective rights to traditional ownership, use, access, occupancy and title to traditional lands, air, forests, waters, oceans, sea ice and sacred sites as well as to ensure that the rights affirmed in Treaties are upheld and recognized in land use planning and climate change mitigation strategies. In particular, States must ensure that Indigenous Peoples have the right to mobility and are not forcibly removed or settled away from their traditional lands and territories, and that the rights of Peoples in voluntary isolation are upheld. In the case of climate change migrants, appropriate programs and measures must address their rights, status, conditions, and vulnerabilities.

12. We call upon states to return and restore lands, territories, waters, forests, oceans, sea ice and sacred sites that have been taken from Indigenous Peoples, limiting our access to our traditional ways of living, thereby causing us to misuse and expose our lands to activities and conditions that contribute to climate change.

13. In order to provide the resources necessary for our collective survival in response to the climate crisis, we declare our communities, waters, air, forests, oceans, sea ice, traditional lands and territories to be *Food Sovereignty Areas*," defined and directed by Indigenous Peoples according to customary

laws, free from extractive industries, deforestation and chemical-based industrial food production systems (i.e. contaminants, agro-fuels, genetically modified organisms).

14. We encourage our communities to exchange information while ensuring the protection and recognition of and respect for the intellectual property rights of Indigenous Peoples at the local, national and international levels pertaining to our Traditional Knowledge, innovations, and practices. These include knowledge and use of land, water and sea ice, traditional agriculture, forest management, ancestral seeds, pastoralism, food plants, animals and medicines and are essential in developing climate change adaptation and mitigation strategies, restoring our food sovereignty and food independence, and strengthening our Indigenous families and nations.

We offer to share with humanity our Traditional Knowledge, innovations, and practices relevant to climate change, provided our fundamental rights as intergenerational guardians of this knowledge are fully recognized and respected. We reiterate the urgent need for collective action.

Agreed by consensus of the participants in the Indigenous Peoples' Global Summit on Climate Change, Anchorage Alaska, April 24th 2009

Jain Faith Statement

This Jain Faith Statement was printed by the ARC, *Alliance of Religion and Conservation,* but was originally printed, along with statements on ecology from ten other faiths, in *Faith in Conservation* by Martin Palmer with Victoria Finlay, published by the World Bank in 2003.

Website: http://www.arcworld.org/faiths.asp?pageID=82d

Dr L. M. Singhvi is President of the Jain Institute, the main body bringing together the three distinct traditions of the Jains. He prepared this statement on behalf of the Institute of Jainology.

> *"Jainism is fundamentally a religion of ecology and has turned ecology into a religion. It has enabled Jains to create an environment-friendly value system and code of conduct."*

The story of Jainism

Jainism is one of the oldest living religions. The term Jain means "follower of the Jinas." The Jinas, or spiritual victors, are human teachers who attained omniscience. They are also called Tirthankaras (ford-makers), those who help others escape the cycle of birth and death. The twenty-fourth Tirthankara, called Mahavira, was born in 599 B.C. At the age of 30, he left home on a spiritual quest. After 12 years of trials and austerities, he attained omniscience. Eleven men became his ganadharas, or chief disciples.

At 72 Mahavira died and attained nirvana, that blissful state beyond life and death. Mahavira was not the founder of a new religion. He consolidated the faith by drawing together the teachings of the previous Tirthankaras, particularly those of his immediate predecessor, Parsva, who lived about 250 years earlier at Varnasi.

Initially the followers of Jainism lived throughout the Ganges Valley in India. Around 250 B.C., most Jains migrated to the city of Mathura on the Yamuna River. Later, many traveled west to Rajasthan and Gujarat and south to Maharashtra and Karnataka, where Jainism rapidly grew in popularity. The Jain population throughout the world is less than 10 million, of which about 100,000 have settled overseas in North America, the United Kingdom, Kenya, Belgium, Singapore, Hong Kong, and Japan.

> *"Asteya"* or "not stealing" is the principle of not taking what belongs to another. It means avoidance of greed and exploitation.

Jain practices

Jains believe that to attain the higher stages of personal development, lay people must adhere to the three jewels (ratna-traya), namely, enlightened worldview, true knowledge, and conduct based on enlightened worldview and true knowledge. They must endeavor to fulfil the anuvratas (small vows). There are five such vows:

Ahimsa (nonviolence)

This is the fundamental vow and runs through the Jain tradition like a golden thread. It involves avoidance of violence in any form through word or deed, not only to human beings but also to all nature. It means reverence for life in every form including plants and animals. Jains practice the principle of compassion for all living beings (Jiva-daya) at every step in daily life. Jains are vegetarians.

Satya (truthfulness)

"Tirthankara Mahavira" (Truth is God) said Sachham Bhagwam.

Asteya (not stealing)

This is the principle of not taking what belongs to another. It means avoidance of greed and exploitation.

Brahmacharya (chastity)

This means practicing restraint and avoiding sexual promiscuity.

Aparigraha (non-materialism)

For lay Jains, this means limiting their acquisition of material goods and contributing one's wealth and time to humanitarian charities and philanthropic causes.

Jain Beliefs

Anekantavada (non-one-sidedness)

This philosophy states that no single perspective on any issue contains the whole truth. It emphasizes the concept of universal interdependence and specifically recommends that one should take into account the viewpoints of other species, other communities and nations, and other human beings.

Loka (the universe)

Space is infinite but only a finite portion is occupied by what is known as the universe. Everything within the universe, whether sentient (jiva) or insentient (ajiva), is eternal, although the forms that a thing may take are transient. Jains preach and practice the principle of the duty of every human being to promote universal well-being (sarva-mangalya).

Jiva (soul)

All living beings have an individual soul (jiva) which occupies the body, a conglomerate of atoms. At the time of death, the soul leaves the body and immediately takes birth in another. Attaining nirvana and thereby terminating this cycle of birth and death is the goal of Jain practice.

Ajiva (non-soul)

Ajiva is everything in the universe that is insentient, including matter, the media of motion and rest, time and space.

Karma

Karma is . . . a form of subtle matter that adheres to the soul as a result of its actions of body, speech, and mind. This accumulated karma is the cause of the soul's bondage in the cycle of birth and death.

Moksha or nirvana (eternal liberation through enlightenment)

The ultimate aim of life is to emancipate the soul from the cycle of birth and death. This is done by exhausting all bound karmas and preventing further accumulation. To achieve moksha, it is necessary to have enlightened worldview, knowledge, and conduct.

Jainism as a Religion of Ecology

Jainism is fundamentally a religion of ecology and has turned ecology into a religion. It has enabled Jains to create an environment-friendly value system and code of conduct. Because of the insistence on rationality in the Jain tradition, Jains are always ready and willing to look positively and with enthusiasm upon environmental causes. In India and abroad, they are in the forefront of bringing greater awareness and putting into practice their cardinal principles on ecology. Their programs have been modest and mostly self-funded through volunteers.

CLIMATE CHANGE

Resolution adopted by the 116th Annual Convention
of the Central Conference of American Rabbis

Houston, TX
March, 2005

Background

In December 1997, the nations of the world gathered in Kyoto, Japan to develop a treaty with binding commitments to address the threat of climate change. The International Panel on Climate Change (IPCC), a group of over 2,000 climate scientists from around the world was charged to evaluate the data on climate change to inform the treaty negotiations. IPCC has documented a number of changes in the earth's atmosphere that are attributed to human activity, causing elevated levels of carbon dioxide and other greenhouse gasses that are heating the earth's surface.

On February 16, 2005, the Kyoto Treaty entered into force, with most of the world's industrialized nations committing to reducing their output of heat trapping carbon emissions. While the Kyoto Protocol represents a monumental step in global cooperation to address an Earth-threatening problem, some environmentalists believe that Kyoto is too-little-too-late. The United States, which produces one quarter of the world's CO_2, while representing only 4 percent of the world's population, is not participating in the Protocol. India and China, developing nations with large populations and fast-paced industrialization, are also not participating. More must be done.

The following Jewish and secular moral principles serve as the foundation for the Conference's position on the development of agreements and policies to address climate change:

Responsibilities to Future Generations: "Therefore choose life, that you and your descendants may live." (Deuteronomy 30:20) Humankind has a solemn obligation to improve the world for future generations. Minimizing climate change requires us to learn how to live within the ecological limits of the Earth, so that we will not compromise the ecological or economic security of those who come after us.

Integrity of Creation: "The human being was placed in the Garden of Eden to till it and to tend it." (Genesis 2:15) Humankind has a solemn obligation to protect the integrity of ecological systems, so that their diverse constituent species, including humans, can thrive.

Equitable Distribution of Responsibility: Nations' responsibilities for reducing greenhouse gas emissions should correlate to their contribution to the problem. The United States has built an economy highly dependent upon fossil fuel use that has affected the entire globe, and must therefore reduce greenhouse gas emissions in a manner that corresponds to its share of the problem.

Protection of the Vulnerable: "When one loves righteousness and justice, the earth is full of the loving-kindness of the Eternal." (Psalm 33:5) The requirements and implementation procedures to address climate change must protect those most vulnerable to climate change both here in the United States and around the globe: poor people, those living in coastal areas, those who rely on subsistence agriculture.

Sustainable Development: The Earth cannot sustain the levels of resource exploitation currently maintained by the developed world. As we work towards global economic development, the developed world should promote the use of renewable energy sources and new technologies, so that developing nations do not face the same environmental challenges that we face today because of industrialization.

Strong action to reduce greenhouse gas emissions is consistent with a number of long-standing public policy priorities, including: improving air quality, increasing mass transit, development of non-polluting alternative energy sources, energy efficiency and energy conservation.

Together, the people of the world can, and must, use our God-given gifts to develop innovative strategies to meet the needs of all who currently dwell on this planet, without compromising the ability of future generations to meet their own needs.

THEREFORE the Central Conference of American Rabbis resolves to:

- Call on the United States Congress to take leadership on the issue of Global Climate Change and support the McCain-Lieberman Climate Stewardship Act. The bill would reduce the dangerously high level of current greenhouse gas pollution by scaling back emissions to year 2000 levels by 2010. By creating a business-friendly design in which unused emissions credits can be bought and sold, the Climate Stewardship Act will have a positive effect on the environment, and will encourage American industry to be more innovative and cost effective, leading to further economic growth;

- Urge the federal government to immediately adopt a variety of policies to accomplish emissions reductions, including: instituting programs that use pricing to lower demand for fossil fuels; encouraging the development of non-polluting energy sources; and raising revenue for public projects such as mass transit, that would lower carbon emissions. Additionally, standards relating to fossil fuel use, such as power plant emissions standards and motor vehicle fuel efficiency standards, should require the use of the most advanced fuel efficiency and emissions reduction technologies available;

- Urge the federal government to complement the above policies with programs to help those Americans whose economic security would be jeopardized by such policies, including assistance to poor people to compensate for increased expenses for electricity, fuel, and transportation and retraining and economic transition assistance for coal miners and other affected workers;

- Urge the federal government to work cooperatively with other nations to address climate change through participation in international bodies, treaties and protocols and through the promotion of international development efforts that promote environmental sustainability; and

- Urge institutions within the Jewish community to promote and provide resources to conduct energy audits of private homes and communal facilities, including synagogues, schools, community centers and commercial buildings and to promote eco-friendly purchasing.

Global Warming: A Jewish Response September, 2000
Coalition on the Environment and Jewish Life (COEJL)
Protecting Creation, Generation to Generation

GLOBAL WARMING:
A Jewish Response

See to it that you do not destroy my world, for there is no one to repair it after you.

Midrash Ecclesiastes Rabbah 7:13

In response to the scientific consensus that human-caused warming of Earth's atmosphere threatens to cause extreme hardship to millions of people around the world and widespread ecological disruption and species extinction:

1. COEJL calls upon Congress and the Administration to move toward the creation of a clean and sustainable energy system for the United States that will significantly reduce greenhouse gas emissions and diminish U.S. reliance on imported oil.

2. COEJL calls upon Jewish institutions and leaders to raise public awareness of the moral and social justice implications of climate change.

3. COEJL calls upon members of the Jewish community, and all other Americans, to institute energy efficiency technologies and practices into private homes and communal facilities and to consider the environment and public health effects of economic decisions, including the purchase of vehicles and appliances and the choice of energy companies.

4. COEJL calls upon the business community to provide leadership in efforts to address global warming.

Contents

Jewish Textual Sources and Suggestions for Taking Action
Global Warming: A Jewish Response September, 2000

BACKGROUND

Since the 1970s, the organized Jewish community has unanimously and consistently supported federal policies and programs to reduce U.S. consumption of fossil fuels. Reliance on fossil fuels compromises our national security by creating dependence upon oil-producing nations, causes and exacerbates illness for millions of our citizens, and degrades our environment. In addition to these historic reasons for supporting reduced use of fossil fuels, today the Jewish community recognizes the world-wide scientific consensus that fossil fuel emissions are significantly contributing to global warming – and that such warming poses grave risks to humankind and the environment. The vast majority of scientists and policy experts agree that if dramatic action is not taken soon, it is very likely that human well-being, global geo-political stability, and the viability of whole ecosystems will be gravely affected by global climate change in the 21st century.

Global warming is largely attributable to the burning of fossil fuels. Industrialized nations, though only one-fifth of the world's population, are responsible for approximately four-fifths of global carbon emissions. The United States has the highest per capita use of energy in the world, using twice as much energy per unit of GNP as its economic equals, such as European countries and Japan. With less than 5 percent of the world's population, the United States is responsible for almost 25 percent of the global carbon emissions. Developing nations, which are expected to emit the majority of global carbon emissions by 2020, are looking to the industrialized world to demonstrate its commitment to reducing its own carbon emissions, which are dramatically higher per capita than in the developing world, before making commitments to cap their own emissions. The leadership demonstrated by the United States is critical to successful efforts to reduce industrial nation and cap developing nation emissions sufficiently to stabilize the climate.

While the world's wealthy nations are most responsible for climate change, communities and nations which are poor, agriculturally marginal, and without adequate medical systems will be most severely impacted. Subsistence farmers are most vulnerable to changing rainfall patterns that may make their land infertile. Slum-dwellers in coastal areas or in floodplains are least able to relocate to avoid chronic flooding. Undeveloped areas are least able to prevent the spread of infectious disease.

The actions taken by industrialized nations to reduce carbon emissions and the choices made by developing nations regarding electricity generation and transportation in the next few years will affect generations to come. Unfortunately, little progress has been made in recent years to curb U.S. reliance on fossil fuels and reduce U.S. greenhouse gas emissions – which continue to rise. In 1999, the average fuel economy of all new passenger vehicles was at its lowest point since 1980, while fuel consumption was at its highest. American vehicle manufacturers lag in bringing new auto technologies to market. And U.S. dependence on foreign oil has grown steadily.

Fortunately, there is a growing consensus among a remarkable cross-section of elected officials, scientists, businesspeople, and religious leaders that we must aggressively address global warming, and that we can do so in a manner that benefits public health, the economy, and the human spirit. Development of environmentally friendly technologies and products will create U.S. jobs, enhance U.S. competitiveness in the global economy, and demonstrate U.S. leadership in the global community. Reduced use of fossil fuels will improve air quality and save lives. And mobilizing broad public participation in the historic effort to create a clean energy economy will build social solidarity and renew the human spirit.

Together, humankind has a solemn obligation to do whatever we can both to prevent harm to current and future generations and to preserve the integrity of the creation with which we have been entrusted. Not to do so when we have the technological capacity – as we do in the case of non-fossil fuel energy and transportation technologies – would be an unforgivable abdication of our responsibility. Together, the people of the world can, and must, use our Godgiven gifts to meet the needs of all who currently dwell on this planet without compromising the ability of future generations to meet their own needs.

PRINCIPLES FOR ACTION

The Coalition on the Environment and Jewish Life believes that the following principles should serve as the foundation for the development of agreements and policies to address climate change:

Responsibilities to Future Generations. Humankind has a solemn obligation to improve the world for future generations. Minimizing climate change requires us to learn how to live within the ecological limits of the earth so that we will not compromise the ecological or economic security of those who come after us.

Integrity of Creation. Humankind has a solemn obligation to protect the integrity of ecological systems so that their diverse constituent species, including humans, can thrive.

Equitable Distribution of Responsibility. Nations' responsibility for reducing greenhouse gas emissions should correlate to their contribution to the problem. The United States has built an economy highly dependent upon fossil fuel use that has affected the entire globe and must therefore reduce greenhouse gas emissions in a manner which accounts for its share of the problem.

Protection of the Vulnerable. The procedures to address climate change must protect those most vulnerable to climate change: poor people, those living in coastal areas, and those who rely on subsistence agriculture.

Energy independence. In recent years, the United States has become increasingly dependent on foreign oil supplies, with important implications for U.S. foreign policy, economic dislocation, and trade deficits. Aggressive measures to wean the U.S. economy from its reliance on fossil fuels will contribute substantially to a secure energy policy.

WE MUST TAKE ACTION TO PREVENT THE POSSIBLE HARMS OF GLOBAL WARMING

Some have said that we should not take measures to address global warming before we are certain that harm will befall humankind. There are many threats to human life that are neither certain nor imminent, and climate change falls into this category.

The Bible provides some instruction for such a case. Deuteronomy 22:8 tells us that, "When you build a new house, you shall make a parapet [a fence] for your roof, so that you do not bring blood-guilt on your house if anyone should fall from it." Rabbi Moses Maimonides, perhaps the greatest Jewish sage, taught that we must take action to protect others from any object of potential danger, by which it is likely that a person could be fatally injured, including building a fence on an unprotected roof. In the Mishneh Torah, his great commentary on the Bible, he wrote that a person (not just the owner) must remove a possible danger that could cause fatal harm to another, even, in the case of the parapet, when the danger is not imminent or certain.

So too with climate change. We must take action to prevent possible danger. It is simply wrong for us to live today in a manner that may well endanger future generations. . . . We stand before choices that will affect generations to come – biblical choices, between life and death, between blessing and curse. Shall energy be a safe, clean, sustainable blessing? Or shall our consumption of energy be a curse, causing harm, and even death, to people and other creatures far into the future?

Excerpted from testimony of Mark X. Jacobs, COEJL's executive director, to the Subcommittee on Transportation and Related Agencies, Committee on Appropriations of the House of Representatives on February 10, 2000. The testimony was in favor of allowing the Department of Transportation to study an increase in fuel economy standards.

PUBLIC POLICY PRIORITIES TO ADDRESS GLOBAL WARMING

Strong action to reduce greenhouse gas emissions is consistent with a number of longstanding public policy priorities of the organized Jewish community, including: improving air quality, increasing mass transit, development of non-polluting alternative energy sources, energy efficiency and energy conservation. COEJL urges the Congress and Administration to:

- Negotiate and ratify binding international agreements, including the Kyoto Protocol, to minimize climate change by committing the United States, other industrialized countries, and developing nations to reducing their current and projected emissions sufficiently to stabilize atmospheric carbon concentrations at a level that will not result in widespread human and/or ecological harm

- Increase Corporate Average Fuel Economy Standards (CAFÉ standards) for all vehicles, and eliminate the loophole that exempts "sport utility vehicles" from conforming to the same standards as cars

- Appropriate foreign aid to developing nations to control carbon emissions

- Appropriate funds and create incentives to effect the rapid adoption of clean and renewable energy sources and technologies, including solar, wind, [and] fuel cell [technologies] and the phasing out of reliance on fossil fuel technologies

- Adopt policies that use pricing – including the taxation of pollution – to lower demand for fossil fuels, encourage the development of non-polluting energy sources, and raise revenue for public projects, such as mass transit, that would lower carbon emissions

- Create programs to help those who live in the United States whose economic security would be jeopardized by changes in energy policy, including assistance to poor people to compensate for increased expenses for electricity, fuel, and transportation and retraining and economic transition assistance for coal miners and other affected workers.

All positions articulated in this document were developed through the Jewish Council for Public Affairs, which serves as the consensus-building body for 13 national and 122 local Jewish public affairs agencies. Contributors to this publication: Mark X. Jacobs, Rabbi Daniel Swartz, Rabbi Larry Troster.

COEJL Participating Organizations

American Jewish Committee, American Jewish Congress, B'nai B'rith International, Coalition for the Advancement of Jewish Education, Hadassah, Hillel, Jewish Community Centers Association, Jewish Council for Public Affairs, Jewish Labor Committee, Jewish National Fund, Jewish Reconstructionist Federation, Jewish Theological Seminary of America, Jewish War Veterans, National Council of Jewish Women, Na'amat USA, New Israel Fund, The Rabbinical Assembly, Reconstructionist Rabbinical Assembly, Religious Action Center of Reform Judaism, The Shalom Center/ALEPH: The Alliance for Jewish Renewal, Union of American Hebrew Congregations, Union of Orthodox Jewish Congregations of America, United Synagogue of Conservative Judaism, U.S.-Israel Environment Council of the American-Israel Friendship League, Women's American ORT, Women of Reform Judaism, Women's League for Conservative Judaism.

Coalition on the Environment and Jewish Life

443 Park Avenue South, 11th floor
New York, NY 10016-7322
tel: 212.684.6950, ext. 210
fax: 212.686.1353
info@coejl.org
www.coejl.org

Lutherans Reflect on Climate Change Conference in Copenhagen

ELCA NEWS SERVICE
December 31, 2009
09-286-JB

CHICAGO (ELCA) — While many who attended or observed the proceedings of the 2009 United Nations Climate Change Conference in Copenhagen this month expressed disappointment in the outcome, others saw the proceedings as an important first step in addressing the effects of climate change—which may lead to more effective action in the future.

Members of the Evangelical Lutheran Church in America (ELCA) and Lutherans from other parts of the world participated in the conference. The Lutheran World Federation (LWF), Geneva, sent a 7-member delegation, which included members from India, Mauritania, Tanzania, the United States and LWF staff.

Mary Minette, director for environmental education and advocacy, ELCA Washington Office, was part of the LWF delegation. Writing a blog while in Copenhagen, she said the LWF delegation expressed concern that "the future of all creation is in jeopardy. Our belief is the issue is not only about science and policy and politics, but also an issue of justice." Minette's blog is at http://www.ELCA.org/advocacy on the ELCA Web site.

More than 3,000 ELCA members, along with a coalition of U.S. faith leaders, sent some 20,000 postcards to President Barack Obama, urging him to be at the meeting, she said. Obama attended the conference and urged leaders of Brazil, China, India and South Africa to join the United States "to fund developing nations' projects to deal with droughts, floods and other impacts of climate change, and to develop clean energy," among other agreements, according to a U.N. news release.

The World Council of Churches, Geneva, criticized the agreement, and in particular cited the "lack of transparency" among those who negotiated it. U.N. Secretary General Ban Ki-Moon urged other nations to sign the agreement.

Minette said the foundation laid by Obama and other world leaders at the conference makes feasible U.S. climate legislation this spring. "The outcome of the conference in Copenhagen is only the start, and the fight against climate change isn't over yet. There is much left to do to ensure the long-term protection of God's good creation," she added.

The Rev. Barbara R. Rossing, professor of New Testament, Lutheran School of Theology at Chicago (LSTC), was part of the LWF delegation. She is a member of the LWF Executive Committee. LSTC is one of eight ELCA seminaries.

Rossing signed an ecumenical statement urging world leaders to be courageous and make "decisions that must be made for all of humanity and for the future of creation." Archbishop Desmond Tutu of South Africa was among those who signed the statement, found at http://bit.ly/6ERjXJ on the Web.

In an ecumenical forum on climate change, Rossing said, "It's the world's poorest people, those who have done the least to cause the problem of climate change, who are the first to suffer its catastrophic effects." She said they ask, "'Why is God punishing us?'"

The Bible can help Christians address the adverse effects of climate change in a positive way, she said. The Book of Revelation, which Rossing has studied and written about extensively, makes clear there is still time to repent for human actions that adversely affect the earth's climate, she said.

Revelation focuses on the urgency of the present moment, Rossing said. She said some scientists have said humanity has less than 10 years to act to significantly reduce carbon emissions before so-called "critical tipping points" are reached on certain environmental concerns.

"We as theologians, ethicists and biblical scholars must take seriously such mounting evidence from science and name this 10-year window as a kind of kairos moment for our churches and for our world—a moment of hope and urgency," Rossing said.

"When this planet is threatened, it is threatened for all of us," the Rev. Olav Fykse Tveit, WCC general secretary-elect, said at the forum. Tveit, a Lutheran, is general secretary, Church of Norway Council on Ecumenical and International Relations. In one way, he said, the climate crisis "brings us together as one humanity."

"Are we able, are we willing to be one church, representing the one humanity with one heart showing the love of the one God for the one world? This is the challenge for the ecumenical movement today and tomorrow," he said.

Rossing's and Tveit's comments can be found at http://bit.ly/6yooqQ on the Web.

The LWF asked its member churches to join people of faith throughout the world to observe Dec. 13 as a day of action for climate change, and to ring bells for climate justice. That same day Archbishop Tutu addressed a rally in Copenhagen, attended by many Lutherans, Rossing said. The Most Rev. Rowan Williams, archbishop of Canterbury and leader of the Anglican Communion, preached at an ecumenical worship service at Copenhagen's Lutheran cathedral.

The ELCA's social statement on the environment, "Caring for Creation: Vision, Hope and Justice," is at http://www.ELCA.org/socialstatements on the ELCA Web site.

Lutherans Restoring Creation

A Resource for the Evangelical Lutheran Church in America

http://www.lutheransrestoringcreation.org/Home/congregations/public-ministry/environmental-justice-and-climate-change-statement

As communities-of-color, Indigenous Peoples, and low-income communities, the Environmental Justice Leadership Forum on Climate Change calls on federal lawmakers and the new president to enact a suite of policies to address Climate Change as an immediate priority. These policies must be just, fair, sustainable and equitable. It is clear that in Congress a cap and trade mechanism has emerged as the leading approach to addressing the Climate Change crisis. Our nation must do better than creating a stock market that commodifies pollution and continues to trade our health and environment for profit.

Climate change is the most significant social and political challenge of the 21st Century, and the time to act is now. In our post hurricanes Katrina and Rita era, we continue to bear witness to an increase in the number of severe weather events impacting communities in the United States. Whether it is the mighty Mississippi River rising along the shores of the Midwest, or the melting permafrost creating displacement in the Arctic, out-of-season record-breaking tornadoes in Mississippi and Kentucky, the burning hills in Sacramento and San Diego or the droughts experienced in Georgia, Tennessee and Alabama, all of these events can be linked in some way to climate change.

Vulnerable communities, even in the most prosperous nations, will be the first and worst hit, as has been confirmed by the United Nations Intergovernmental Panel on Climate Change. In the U.S. context this includes communities-of-color, Indigenous Peoples, and low-income communities that are socio-economically disadvantaged, disproportionately burdened by poor environmental quality and least able to adapt.

The scientific debate on climate change has shifted from uncertainty about the drivers of this phenomenon to clear confidence that human activity, specifically the fossil-fuel and carbon-intensive way we power our modern economy, is a central culprit or accelerant in the changes in the climate or what we call global warming. Scientists and policymakers concur that climate change and global warming will result in far-ranging effects on human health, and indeed sociopolitical and economic stability. Evidence of these impacts are documented by the World Health Organization that reports tens of thousands have been displaced in developed countries by recent severe weather events.

The history of this country is one of struggles to achieve equity, justice and opportunity. Each generation has faced this political challenge. In this moment we are confronted with the real possibility of climate change stealing the American ideal of opportunity from not just low-income Americans, not just Indigenous Peoples, not just persons-of-color in America, but all Americans. The Environmental Justice Forum on Climate Change calls on Congress to develop policies to combat climate change that: (words missing on website)

Environmental Justice Leadership Forum on Climate Change

PRINCIPLES OF CLIMATE JUSTICE

1. Establish a zero carbon economy and achieve this by limiting and reducing greenhouse gas emissions in accordance with the levels advocated by the scientific community (25% by 2020 and 80% by 2050) through mechanisms that are controlled by the public sector, generate revenue, are transparent, easily understandable by all, can be set up quickly and have a track record of improving environmental quality;

2. Protect all of America's people—regardless of race, gender, nationality, or socioeconomic status—and their communities equally from the environmental, health and social impacts of climate change. Ensure that any solutions implemented to respond to or mitigate climate change do not violate human or environmental rights;

3. Ensure that carbon reduction strategies do not negatively impact public health and do not further exacerbate existing health disparities among communities. This includes crafting strategies that prevent the creation of pollution hotspots, eliminate existing emissions hotspots in vulnerable communities, and reduce the emissions of greenhouse gas co-pollutants in and near communities-of-color, Indigenous, and low-income communities;

4. Require those most responsible for creating the impacts that arise from climate change to bear the proportionate cost of responding to the resulting economic, social and environmental crisis. In setting the proportionate cost of climate-impacting activity, the full environmental, health, social and economic cost of energy use from extraction to disposal must be included to accurately reflect the cost that energy use inflicts on our environment, our health and our communities;

5. Develop a national goal supported by legislatively dedicated resources to transition us from the fossil fuel economy to a green, clean renewable energy economy by 2020;

6. Position the public sector to be a catalyst for change in the transition to the green, clean renewable energy economy by dedicating some of the revenues generated by carbon reduction strategies to support green clean renewable energy initiatives;

7. Create the opportunity for all Americans, especially people-of-color, Indigenous Peoples and low-income Americans, to experience a just transition as well as to participate in the creation and operation of a new green economy by creating a workforce development program to grow living-wage, clean, safe, green jobs in the energy sector and beyond;

8. Provide an economic and social safety net for low-income persons, people-of-color, Indigenous Peoples and those vulnerable in the middle-income bracket from structural adjustments in the economy as we transition from the pollution generating fossil fuel economy to the green, clean and renewable economy;

9. Ensure that the green economy has enough jobs for those who need to be retrained and those who historically have been chronically underemployed, unemployed and/or excluded from unions; and

10. Ensure that people-of-color, Indigenous Peoples and low-income communities, who are and continue to be disproportionately impacted by climate change, have the inalienable right to have our voices shape what is the most significant policy debate of the 21st Century.

The Environmental Justice Leadership Forum on Climate Change believes that climate change policies that incorporate these principles are the way forward for the United States of America to restore our credibility nationally and globally on the issue of climate change while preserving the livelihoods, health and safety of all Americans.

Global Warming and Energy

From: General Board of Church & Society of United Methodist Church Website: http://www.umc-gbcs.org/site/apps/nl/content3.asp?c=frLJK2PKLqF&b=3631781&ct=3956191
[possibly posted sometime in 2008]

"The earth lies polluted under its inhabitants; for they have transgressed laws, violated the statutes, broken the everlasting covenant."   Isaiah 24, NRSV

Background

The crisis facing God's earth is clear. We, as stewards, have failed to live into our responsibility to care for creation and have instead abused it in ways that now threaten life around the planet.

The scientific consensus is clear that human activities are leading to a warming of the surface temperatures of the planet and the effects of this warming are being felt now and will be felt more intensely in years to come.

As a matter of stewardship and justice, Christians must take action now to reduce global warming pollution and stand in solidarity with our brothers and sisters around the world whose lands, livelihoods and lives are threatened by the global climate crisis.

Biblical and Theological Context

"The scale of human activity has grown so large that it now threatens the planet itself. Global environmental problems have become so vast they are hard to comprehend. . . . The vast majority of scientific evidence suggests that carbon dioxide from fossil fuels has already caused a measurable warming of the globe. Confronted with the massive crisis of the deterioration of God's creation and faced with the question of the ultimate survival of life, we ask God's forgiveness for our participation in this destruction." (2004 Book of Resolutions, "Environmental Justice for a Sustainable Future," ¶7)

"A transition to energy efficiency and renewable energy sources will combat global warming, protect human health, create new jobs, and ensure a secure, affordable energy future." (2004 Book of Resolutions, "Energy Policy Statement," ¶5)

"The United States must move beyond its dependence on high carbon fossil fuels that produce emissions leading to climate change and ratify the Kyoto Protocol under the U.N. Framework Convention on Climate Change." (2004 Book of Resolutions, "U.S. Energy Policy and United Methodist Responsibility," ¶6)

Scripture references: Isaiah 24:4-5 and 2 Chronicles 7:14

What GBCS is Doing

The General Board of Church and Society (GBCS) advocates for the United States to adopt mandatory global warming emissions reductions and re-engage in the global dialogue and international framework for combating this clear and present danger. In collaboration with ecumenical and interfaith allies, GBCS supports a climate and energy campaign that focuses on both state and federal action. In addition, GBCS provides educational and worship resources to bring this issue into the life of the church.

Methodists Commit to Carbon Reduction Pledge

From: The Methodist Conference Website:
http://www.methodistconference.org.uk/news/latest-news/methodists-commit-to-carbon-reduction-pledge
[probably posted sometime in 2011]

The Methodist Conference agreed that failure to acknowledge the urgent need for radical cuts in greenhouse gas emissions was "morally irresponsible" in a statement adopted by the Church today.

The statement has been two years in the making. In 2009 a report entitled "Hope in God's Future" addressed the need to look at climate change within a theological context. Over the past year, British Methodists have been asked about their views on climate change in a Church-wide consultation. Now that the statement has been adopted, it will stand as the official view of the Church and be referred to by key committees, such as the Faith and Order Committee, when deciding on related areas of doctrine.

Dr. Richard Vautrey, former Vice President of the Methodist Church, said: "The scientific analyses of climate change and the role of human greenhouse gas emissions are well grounded. It is now morally irresponsible to fail to acknowledge and address the urgent need for radical cuts in greenhouse gas emissions in order to prevent intolerable damage to human populations and mass extinctions of many plant and animal species."

This week the Church launched a webpage on how to reduce the carbon footprint of small, medium and large churches. The guidance will help to cut the Methodist Church's carbon emissions by 80 per cent by 2050 in line with Government targets. A report to the Methodist Conference last year revealed that the Methodist Church in Britain has a carbon footprint of around 120,000 tonnes of CO_2 per annum for approximately 8,000 of its buildings.

The Joint Public Issues Team for the Methodist Church, the United Reformed Church and the Baptist Union is lobbying the government on its climate change policy and has called for emissions from international aviation and shipping to be taken into account in international targets. Churches are also encouraged to start up eco-congregations: an environmental programme for local churches in Britain and Ireland. Last week, Nailsea Methodist Church was officially named as an Eco-Congregation after four years of working towards a greener church.

Islamic Faith Statement

http://www.arcworld.org/This statement was printed by the ARC, *Alliance of Religion and Conservation*, but was originally printed, along with Statements from ten other faiths, in *Faith in Conservation* by Martin Palmer with Victoria Finlay, published by the World Bank in 2003 http://www.arcworld.org/ . Website: http://www.arcworld.org/faiths.asp?pageID=75

Hyder Ihsan Mahasneh is a biologist and Islamic scholar and was the first African head of the Kenya National Parks Service. He was appointed by the Muslim World League to compile this paper.

> O children of Adam! . . . eat and drink: but waste not by excess for Allah loveth not the wasters.

Humans and the Environment

Humanity's most primordial concepts of religion relate to the environment. Human history on planet Earth is, on a geological scale, very short indeed. Planet Earth itself is a mere 3,800 million years old; human beings only appeared one million or maybe two million years ago.

Most of the physical patterns of planet Earth were probably in place, broadly speaking, by the time humans evolved. Apart from what they first saw, they also probably witnessed some spectacular changes themselves. They must, at the very least, have gone through one Ice Age and seen some graphic volcanic eruptions—assuming they were able to avoid the consequences. The environment, therefore, very probably induced the first thoughts of a Super-Being—a God, if you like—whose manifestations lay in human beings' immediate surroundings.

The environment also provided another dimension in humanity's relationship with nature. To survive in a given environment, humans have to adjust what they take from that environment to what can give them sustainable yields on (at the very least) an annual basis. In effect this meant that early humans had to learn to conserve at an early age. Being largely dependent on what was available rather than on what they could cultivate, they entered into a partnership with the environment.

To take more than the regenerative capacity of the environment could lead to serious subsequent exhaustion—quite rightly seen as harsh retribution from an angry God. The converse situation of exploitation with moderation led to sustained yields, which were (again, quite rightly) taken as having pleased God.

The Industrial Revolution

This relationship between conservation and religion is thus not only a natural one but also probably as old as the proverbial hills. But when we quickly open most of the pages of human history on planet Earth and come to the past 300 years or so, we find the advent of the Industrial Revolution. It made possible the production of large quantities of goods in a very short time. That meant that raw materials in ever-increasing quantities had to be found to feed the hungry mills ready to convert them into finished or semi-finished goods.

> Behold thy Lord said to the angels: "I will create a vice-regent on earth." They said "Wilt thou place therein one who will make mischief therein and shed blood? Whilst we do celebrate Thy praises and glorify Thy holy [name]?" He said: "I know what ye know not."

The consequences were many—economic, social, and environmental. The material achievements of the human race in the past 100 or so years have overshadowed the contributions made by all past civilizations.

The Industrial Revolution that took place in Europe in the eighteenth and nineteenth centuries exacted a high social and environmental cost. Now these costs are even higher and more universal, being manifestly so in the great urban centers of the world. The paradox of "progress" today is the easily perceived correlation between complex consumer societies and the degeneration of the human being. Or as John Seymour puts it:

> We see men now wherever we look, so blinded by arrogance and the worship of man as God that they are doing things no one but the insane would do . . . men maddened by the belief that they are both omniscient and omnipotent, that they are indeed God.

The pursuit of money

The Industrial Revolution also proclaimed a new revival of another God: Mammon. Mammon regrettably has no respect for environmental integrity—nor do his followers. The last 250 years have seen a growing decimation of ever more pristine areas of nature to feed the insatiable industrial cuckoo and its resultant consumerism. Forests—particularly tropical forests—have been systematically hewn down, the seas ransacked, the lands made totally dependent on a host of inorganic fertilizers and pesticides for food production. Wastes galore have filled the seas, the rivers, and the lakes, not to mention the landfills.

We must also take note that the "unmatched material progress" of this century that we are often fond of talking about has only been possible for the few: that is, the population of the northern hemisphere and a small minority among the peoples of the South. This is usually translated as less than 25 percent of the world's population consuming over 75 percent of the world's resources.

This rate of consumption by a minority of the human species has caused unparalleled climatic change, ecosystem disintegration, and species extinction. As a report by the World Wide Fund for Nature observes, loss of biodiversity worldwide, and the combination of global warming with other human pressures will present the greatest challenge in conservation for decades to come.

This would lead us to conclude that there is a profound and inherent contradiction in the efforts made by the "North" to keep ahead of the rest as consumers, and the push by the remaining 75 percent of the world's population to catch up. Given this scenario, if just Eastern Europe or Russia or India or China managed to raise its standard of living by just a few percentage points, then the consequences of putting this extra load on the earth's ecosystem, which is already under severe strain, would be catastrophic.

This is the background against which the followers of the relatively ancient, environmentally conscious (indeed environmentally concerned) God have gathered to reexamine and to restate their own commitment to environmental integrity from their own individual religions' standpoint. We for our part will look at the underpinnings of conservation in Islam.

Islam and conservation

There are several Islamic principles that, when taken individually, seem to have little bearing on conservation. Together, however, they add up to a clear concept of the Islamic view on conservation.

Muslim

Tawheed

The first Islamic principle that relates to conservation is that of the Oneness of Allah, or Tawheed. This principle is absolutely fundamental to Islam. Every Muslim must believe in this Oneness of Allah. It is said by some Ulamaa that some two-thirds of Prophet Muhammad's (SAW) early preaching—and indeed of the Qur'an itself—were and are dedicated purely to endorsing this very Oneness of Allah. One indivisible God means to a Muslim that there is no separate deity for each of the many attributes that to Muslims belong to the One Universal God who is also God of the Universe.

Tawheed is the monotheistic principle of Islam and it begins by declaring that "there is no God but God" (the second half of this declaration asserts that "Muhammad is His Messenger"). We are for the present concerned with the first part, which affirms that there is nothing other than the Absolute, the Eternal, All Powerful Creator. This is the bedrock statement of the Oneness of the Creator from which stems everything else.

It is the primordial testimony of the unity of all creation and the interlocking grid of the natural order of which man is intrinsically a part.

God says in the Qur'an:

> Say: He is Allah the One and Only; Allah the Eternal Absolute; He begetteth not nor is He begotten; And there is none like unto Him. (112.001-4) . . . God is Real, not an abstract idea or concept; He is One, the Everlasting Refuge for all creation.

Man's relation to God

The emphasis on Tawheed is significant in itself but it is even more relevant to the present discussion by virtue of defining a Muslim's relationship to Allah. The Omniscience and Omnipotence of Allah means, by definition, that a Muslim's relationship to Allah is total. To Him—and to Him only—should humans refer for all their needs: physical, mental, and spiritual. Indeed, Allah would not have it any other way. As He says in the Qur'an:

> Allah forgiveth not that partners should be set up with him; but He forgiveth anything else to whom He pleaseth; to set up partners with Allah is to devise a sin most heinous in deed. 004.048.

But Allah is not only the One Indivisible God. He is also the Universal God as well as the Lord of the Universe:

> Praise be to Allah, Lord of the Worlds. 001.002.

And again:

> Say: "Allah's guidance is the [only] guidance and we have been directed to submit ourselves to the Lord of the worlds. . . . To establish regular prayers and to fear Allah; for it is to Him that we shall be gathered together. . . . It is He Who created the heavens and the earth in true [proportions]: the day He saith "Be" Behold! it is. His Word is the truth. His will be the dominion the day the trumpet will be blown. He knoweth the Unseen as well as that which is open. For He is the Wise well acquainted [with all things]. 006.071-3.

To Allah belong the earth and the heavens

Yet another principle that underpins Islamic commitment to the conservation of nature and natural resources is the principle of divine ownership of all that exists on earth and in the heavens—animate and inanimate. There are countless verses in the Holy Qur'an that state this. A few are given below.

In the celebrated Ayatul Kursiyy:

> Allah! There is no Allah but He the living the Self subsisting Eternal. No slumber can seize him nor sleep. His are all things in the heavens and on earth. Who is there can intercede in His presence except as He permitteth? He knoweth what [appeareth to his creatures as] before or after or behind them. Nor shall they compass aught of his knowledge except as He willeth. His throne doth extend over the heavens and the earth and He feeleth no fatigue in guarding and preserving them. For He is the Most High the Supreme [in glory]. 002.255.

And again:

> To Him belong all things in the heavens and on earth. And enough is Allah as a Disposer of affairs. 004.171

> To Him belongeth all that dwelleth [or lurketh] in the night and the day. For He is the One Who heareth and knoweth all things. 006.013.

> To Him belongs what is in the heavens and on earth and all between them and all beneath the soil. 020.006.

> To Him belong all [creatures] in the heavens and on earth: even those who are in His [very] Presence are not too proud to serve Him nor are they [ever] weary [of His service)]. 021.019.

But we are reminded that all things animate and inanimate, in their own ways, submit themselves to the Glory of Allah. There are many verses in the Qur'an about this:

> To Him belongs every being that is in the heavens and on earth: all are devoutly obedient to Him. 030.026.

And again:

> Whatever is in the heavens and on earth doth declare the Praises and Glory of Allah the Sovereign the Holy One the Exalted in Might the Wise.062.001.

Thus Allah, the One Indivisible God, the Universal God and the Lord of the Universe is the Owner also of all that is in the universe, including man. After all, we are reminded to say constantly:

> Be sure We shall test you with something of fear and hunger some loss in goods or lives or the fruits [of your toil] but give glad tidings to those who patiently persevere.

> Who say when afflicted with calamity: "To Allah we belong and to Him is our return." 002.155-6

The above set of principles—all taken from Islam's ultimate authority, the Holy Qu'ran—define the perspectives of the relationship of humanity to God and of God to the environment in its totality. A second set of principles that the Holy Qur'an enunciates prescribe man's relationship to the environment after, of course, humanity has accepted the preceding principles.

Man and the Khalifa

The most important of this second set of principles is that which defines the human role and responsibilities in the natural order that Allah provided. The appointment of people as Khalifa, or guardians, is the sacred duty God has given to the human race. The appointment of humanity to this elevated position gives rise to the one occasion when the Angels actually questioned Allah's decision as seen in the following verses:

> Behold thy Lord said to the angels: "I will create a vice-regent on earth." They said "Wilt thou place therein one who will make mischief therein and shed blood? Whilst we do celebrate Thy praises and glorify Thy holy [name]?" He said: "I know what ye know not."

> And He taught Adam the nature of all things; then He placed them before the angels and said: "Tell Me the nature of these if ye are right."

> They said: "Glory to Thee of knowledge we have none save that Thou hast taught us: in truth it is Thou who art perfect in knowledge and wisdom."

> He said: "O Adam I tell them their natures." When he had told them Allah said: "Did I not tell you that I know the secrets of heaven and earth and I know what ye reveal and what ye conceal?"

> And behold We said to the angels: "Bow down to Adam"; and they bowed down, not so Iblis he refused and was haughty he was of those who reject Faith.002.030-34

Clearly Allah preferred unprogrammed free will of humanity to the pre-programmed goodness of Angels!

And again:

> It is He who hath made you [His] agents inheritors of the earth: He hath raised you in ranks some above others: that he may try you in the gifts He hath given you: for thy Lord is·quick in punishment: yet He is indeed Oft-Forgiving Most Merciful. 006.165.

The exercise of the vice regency is defined in the Qur'an by another set of principles in which man's privileges as well as his responsibilities are clearly defined.

Mizaan

One of the most important attributes conferred on human beings is the faculty of reasoning. This, above all, might well be the deciding fact in their appointment as God's vice regents on earth. Here are the relevant verses:

> [Allah] Most Gracious!
> It is He Who has taught the Qur'an.
> He has created man:
> He has taught him speech [and Intelligence]

The sun and the moon follow courses [exactly] computed;
And the herbs and the trees—both [alike] bow in adoration.
And the firmament has He raised high and He has set up the balance [of Justice]
In order that ye may not transgress [due] balance.
So establish weight with justice and fall not short in the balance.
It is He Who has spread out the earth for [His] creatures:
Therein is fruit and date-palms producing spathes [enclosing dates]:
Also corn with [its] leaves and stalk for fodder and sweet-smelling plants.
Then which of the favors of your Lord will ye deny? (055.001-013)

Humans were not created to function exclusively on instinct. The "explanation" was taught to us because we had the capacity to reason and understand.

There is order and purpose in the whole pattern of creation. The Sun and Moon following stable orbits make life possible. The whole universe is in submission to the Creator—the stars that enable us to steer courses and the trees that give us sustenance, shelter and other uses. The world functions only because creation follows a preordained pattern. Man then has a responsibility by virtue of being able to reason, to behave justly, "to transgress not in the balance." We owe this to ourselves as much as to the rest of creation.

Justice

The capacity to reason and to balance intellectual judgment would in itself be insufficient without the additional moral commitment to Justice. And this is what the Qur'an prescribes for Muslims:

O ye who believe! Stand out firmly for justice as witnesses to Allah even as against yourselves or your parents or your kin and whether it be [against] rich or poor: for Allah can best protect both. Follow not the lusts [of your hearts] lest ye swerve and if ye distort [justice] or decline to do justice verily Allah is well acquainted with all that ye do. 004.135.

And again:

Whoever recommends and helps a good cause becomes a partner therein: and whoever recommends and helps an evil cause shares in its burden: and Allah hath power over all things. 004.085.

Allah doth command you to render back your trusts to those to whom they are due; and when ye judge between man and man that ye judge with justice: verily how excellent is the teaching which He giveth you! for Allah is He who heareth and seeth all things. 004.058

And again:

O ye who believe! stand out firmly for Allah as witnesses to fair dealing and let not the hatred of others to you make you swerve to wrong and depart from justice. Be just: that is next to Piety: and fear Allah for Allah is well-acquainted with all that ye do.005.009.

[They are fond of] listening to falsehood, of devouring anything forbidden. If they do come to thee either judge between them or decline to interfere. If thou decline they cannot hurt thee in the least. If thou judge judge in equity between them; for Allah loveth those who judge in equity.005.045.

Muslim

Use but do not abuse

Several times in the Qur'an, man is invited to make use of the nourishing goods that Allah has placed on earth for him, but abuse—particularly through extravagance and excess—is strictly forbidden. Sometimes these principles are stated in one breath, so to speak. Sometimes they are stated separately. But the message is the same, as the following verse indicates:

> O children of Adam! . . . eat and drink: but waste not by excess for Allah loveth not the wasters. 007.031.

There are as many invitations to partake of nature as provided for man and for other creatures of the earth as there are for the avoidance of wasteful extravagance. Time and again, Allah reminds us that He loveth not wasters.

> It is He who produceth gardens with trellises and without and dates and tilth with produce of all kinds and olives and pomegranates similar [in kind] and different [in variety]: eat of their fruit in their season but render the dues that are proper on the day that the harvest is gathered. But waste not by excess: for Allah loveth not the wasters. 006.141.

Fitra

Fitra can be taken as perhaps the most direct injunction by Allah to man to conserve the environment and not to change the balance of His creation. This is specifically contained in the verse below:

> So set thou thy face steadily and truly to the Faith: [Establish] Allah's handiwork according to the pattern on which He has made mankind: no change [let there be] in the work [wrought] by Allah: that is the standard Religion: but most among mankind understand not. 030.030.

Thus, Islam teaches that humanity is an integral part of the environment; it is part of the creation of Almighty God. We remain deeply locked into the natural domain despite the fact that there is talk of bringing the environment to the people as though we were independent of it.

The power given to man by God is seen in Islam to be limited by the responsibilities he bears, not only toward God and other men and women, but also toward the rest of creation.

Seyyed Hossein Nasr says: *"The Divine Law (al shariah) is explicit in extending the religious duties of man to the natural order and the environment."*

Conclusion

As we indicated at the beginning, there are several Qur'anic principles that, taken separately, do not have an obvious connection with conservation. But taken in their totality, they state in clear terms that Allah, the One True God is the Universal God and the Creator of the Universe and indeed, the Owner of the Universe. To Him belong all the animate and inanimate objects, all of whom should or do submit themselves to Him.

Allah, in His Wisdom, appointed humans, the creatures that He has conferred with the faculty of reason and with free will, to be His vice regents on earth. And while Allah has invited people to partake of the fruits of the earth for their rightful nourishment and enjoyment, He has also directed them not to waste that which Allah has provided for him—for He loveth not wasters.

Furthermore, Allah has also ordered humans to administer his responsibilities with Justice. Above all, people should conserve the balance of Allah's creation on Earth. By virtue of their intelligence, humanity (when it believes in the One Universal Allah, the Creator of the Universe) is the only creation of Allah to be entrusted with the overall responsibility of maintaining planet Earth in the overall balanced ecology that man found.

If biologists believe that humans are the greatest agents of ecological change on the surface of the earth, is it not humans who, drawn from the brink, will—for their own good—abandon Mammon and listen to the prescriptions of God on the conservation of their environment and the environment of all the creatures on earth? The Islamic answer to this question is decisively in the affirmative.

Statement on Global Climate Change & Stewardship of the Earth
Presbyterian Church (U.S.A.) – Synod of the Trinity
Statement on Global Climate Change [c. 1990]

WHEREAS

God created the earth and all that is within it, and
We are directed by God to be stewards of the earth both for its own sake and so that present and future generations may live and enjoy its fruits, and
As members of Christ's Church we are called to exhibit to the world around us Christ's offer of redemption and reconciliation to humankind and to all of creation;

AND WHEREAS

- We all have sinned and fallen short of the glory of God, and
- Human activity is the realm in which we live out either God's sovereign plan or our fallen human nature, and
- The links between human activity, increasing concentrations of greenhouse gases in the atmosphere, and rising global temperature and sea level are well established, and
- Global temperature and sea level are expected to rise unless we take steps to substantially reduce greenhouse gas emissions so that concentrations are stabilized, and
- Climate change and sea level rise are apt to affect everyone and everything: food, water, air quality, biodiversity, forests, public health, social order and world peace, and
- The poor, the young, and the elderly are often the most vulnerable when weather-related and climate-related disasters strike;

AND WHEREAS

- Our first obligation is to discern and do God's will, and
- Since 1990 the General Assembly of the Presbyterian Church (USA) has urged the U.S. government to take the lead in addressing global warming through international agreements and domestic policies to increase energy conservation and efficiency, and to accelerate the transition to safe, non-polluting, affordable energy, and
- The General Assembly has also urged its congregations to engage in education about global warming, and encouraged congregations to take measures to increase energy conservation and efficiency, and
- Representatives of the Presbyterian Church (USA) have been instrumental in developing interfaith climate campaigns in eighteen states.
- The Synod of the Trinity, comprised of the eastern counties of Ohio, all of Pennsylvania, and most of West Virginia, has signed and supports The Religious Leaders' Statements in support of their respective state campaigns.

Now Therefore Be It Resolved That
We, the Synod of The Trinity, Meeting in the Month of October in the Year 2001, Urge Our Presbyteries and Congregations to Participate in the Interfaith Global Climate Change Campaign of the Ohio, Pennsylvania and West Virginia Councils of Churches by:

- Seeking guidance through prayer and the study of Scripture for wisdom and strength as we seek to address the human activities that do violence to the integrity of God's creation by causing global climate change,
- Providing education by using the resources available through the Campaign to help members of congregations understand and embrace the challenge of global warming as a religious issue,
- Examining opportunities to reduce greenhouse emissions by using less energy, increasing energy efficiency, and buying electricity that comes partly or entirely from renewable sources,
- Supporting the Pennsylvania Council of Churches' activities to address global climate change in national and state policies, while understanding that the obligation to restore the integrity of God's creation must transcend partisan politics,
- Thanking God for the good gift of creation through our stewardship of it, and always remembering to be grateful for what God has done for us.

Restoring Creation for Ecology and Justice
Presbyterian Church (U.S.A.) Statement on Global Climate Change
an excerpt from the 1990 General Assembly policy paper

5. Area Five: Overcoming Atmospheric Instability – Global Warming and Ozone Depletion.

Background information on ozone depletion and global warming may be found in Part I of this report, in "Keeping and Healing the Creation," pp. 21-25, and in *Church and Society* Magazine (March/April 1990).

We note that the phenomena determining climate are very complex and that scientific opinion varies with respect to the reliability of models projecting temperature increases. The weight of evidence, however, justifies a serious response to the threat of global warming.

Ozone depletion and global warming have risen rapidly to head the list of concerns about the future of creation. They are significantly different from other problems in several respects. They have to do with global problems that lie ahead and cannot now be measured. No place on earth will be unaffected, however. Without united action worldwide, no nation can do much about global warming and ozone depletion. They represent the unintended consequences of proud industrial achievements. The gases released were not toxic. Chlorofluorocarbons (CFCs) have had all sorts of beneficial uses, and we breathe air with CO_2 in it. Now in the upper atmosphere these gases are doing enormous damage. But we cannot get them down again. We can only stop sending them up and thereby limit the damage.

In the case of CO_2, substantial reduction of emissions means changing the energy basis of our whole civilization. We knew that fossil fuels would not last indefinitely; but suddenly the danger is that they will last too long, that the world will not make the transition soon enough to simpler, more efficient, and renewable energy sources and technologies.

In August 1989, the United Church of Canada and eight European churches came to a "Covenantal Agreement Regarding the Threat of Global Warming." They did this in connection with the meeting in Basel, Switzerland, of Protestant and Catholic Christians from East and West Europe on the Justice, Peace, and Integrity of Creation theme of the World Council of Churches. They agreed to work together on the problem of global warming and to give particular attention to the role of energy. They have already made an important approach to governments by advocating cooperation on reduction in the use of fossil fuels by means of energy-saving technologies and the development of renewable (solar) energy supplies. They presented comments and policy statements to the October 1989 environmental meeting in Sofia, Bulgaria, of governments belonging to the Conference on Security and Cooperation in Europe.

These are significant developments. An invitation has come to U.S. churches, through their representatives on the NCC Eco-Justice Working Group and through their delegates to the 1990 World Convocation on JPIC in Seoul, Korea, to participate in this international cooperative effort of churches on global warming.

The 202nd General Assembly (1990) recommends:

1. Ecumenical Participation and International Participation

1. The Presbyterian Church (USA) declares its serious concern, in concert with ecumenical partners, that the global atmospheric warming trend (the greenhouse effect) represents one of the most serious global environmental challenges to the health, security, and stability of human life and natural ecosystems; and
2. The church affirms its intention to participate in ecumenical efforts to address this challenge cooperatively with Canadian and European churches and the conciliar movement.
3. The General Assembly affirms its intention to participate in the United Nations International Conference on Environment and Development, to be held in 1992, and requests a report to a subsequent General Assembly as appropriate.

2. Policies on Global Warming

    a. The United States, as consumer of nearly a quarter of the world's energy, must take the lead in reducing its own combustion of fossil fuels and shifting to renewable sources of energy which do not contribute to the atmospheric buildup of carbon dioxide.

b. Appropriate response to the warnings of impending climate change requires an extended frame of reference for decision making by governments, international agencies, industries, educational institutions, churches, and community organizations. The U.S. government, other governments, the United Nations, and appropriate scientific organizations should increase their capability to monitor and project trends in atmospheric temperature and to make broad environmental and social assessments.

c. The United States should work through the United Nations and appropriate diplomatic channels to reach firm international agreements and for halting deforestation and promoting reforestation. Some programs already in place should be given an enlarged role and increased funding—the U.N. Environment Programme, for example, and the U.N.'s programs on development and population.

d. The United States government should adopt legislation and administrative policies, with adequate funding, for vigorously stepped-up research and development and energy-efficient technologies.

e. The U.S. government should promote the introduction and use of energy-efficient technologies by applying carefully targeted incentives and disincentives.

f. Similarly, the U.S. government should adopt legislation and administrative policies, with adequate funding, to step up research and development on the various sources and technologies for social energy. Appropriate incentives and disincentives to accelerate the transition to an economy based on renewable, safe, nonpolluting, affordable energy should be developed and implemented.

g. The United States and other industrialized nations should assist developing countries to achieve the energy sufficiency necessary for the general improvement of living standards that these countries desperately need. This assistance should include appropriate technology transfers for pollution control and energy efficiency. In particular, assistance will be necessary to enable developing countries to find equitable solutions to the problems of debt and land use that figure heavily in the destruction of their forests.

h. The U.S. Environmental Protection Agency should act promptly to strengthen fuel economy and emission standards for automobiles, buses, and trucks by mandating and consistently enforcing a schedule of energy efficiency improvements, leading to a substantially higher standard of efficiency within a few years. Incentive and disincentives to encourage consumers to choose fuel-efficient vehicles will also be in order.

i. Comparable standard-setting and incentive-generating measures should be advanced by the U.S. Bureau of Standards with respect to efficiency improvements in lighting, heating, air conditioning, appliances, building construction, the weatherization of existing buildings, and the co-generation of heat and electricity (with legislation as necessary where the bureau's powers do not apply). As more efficient technologies become available, public policy should encourage and facilitate their adoption and use by individuals and businesses.

j. Public policy should encourage alternatives to private automobiles. Alternatives include municipal mass transit, railroads, bicycles, and walking.

3. Policies on Ozone Depletion

To a large extent the kinds of policies needed for reducing the emissions of chlorofluorocarbons (CFCs) and other ozone-destroying gases parallel the policies required for reducing the buildup of the greenhouse gases. CFCs not only are the leading cause of ozone depletion but also add significantly to the greenhouse effect. To protect the ozone shield, there is clearly need for international action through

- leadership by the United States, which is the largest contributor to the problem;

- a longer-term and global frame of reference, with improved foresight capability by governments and international agencies;

- strong international agreements and cooperative arrangements; specifically, firm adherence to the Montreal and Helsinki agreements on phasing out the production of CFCs by the end of the century and discontinuing the other ozone-destroying chemicals as soon as possible, with continuing efforts to bring additional nations into the pact;

- improved technologies and development of acceptable substitutes for the chemicals that must be phased out; rapid shifts in production processes;

- assistance to developing countries by providing them with information, training, funding mechanisms, and technology transfers that will enable them to participate in the Montreal-Helsinki pact and have access to the improved technologies and substitute chemicals;

- strict standards, in line with international agreements but enforced by governments;

- incentives and disincentives that lead actors in a market economy to make environmentally rational decisions.

4. Church Support through Personal and Institutional Practice

- The American people, beginning with members of our churches, must be challenged to form personal habits consistent with the need to cut back on the emissions of the gases that are causing the greenhouse effect and the depletion of the ozone layer. This means energy conservation and cutting back on the use of fossil fuel energy. It means avoiding foams made with CFCs and making sure that CFC-based coolant is not released when air conditioners are serviced.

- The greenhouse and ozone problems reinforce the call to a less materialistic and wasteful style of life. It is unrealistic and self serving to think that efficient and renewable technologies, now in the early stage of the transition, will take effect fast enough to provide sufficient insurance against the potentially disastrous consequences of global warming—unless there is also a move away from unnecessary and wasteful production and consumption.

- The church in its own life must teach, exemplify, and advocate the values and principles, policies and practices that break down the ozone. Obviously the church must be responsible in the construction and maintenance of its own buildings. If habits of conservation and responsible consuming are cultivated consistently, we shall discover many practical applications of our values.

As this report has repeatedly made clear, the affliction of the creation will not be healed unless the human part of creation undergoes significant personal and institutional transformation. Our recommendations suggest something of what the transformation may entail, but they fall far short of prescribing all that is needed. That will be the agenda for the coming years.

About the Responsibility to Address Global Climate Change
Society of Friends Statement on Global Climate Change

At the June 2000 session of Interim Meeting, Philadelphia Yearly Meeting approved this minute on the responsibility to address global climate change:

Protecting God's Earth and its fullness of life is of fundamental religious concern to the Society of Friends. The links between human activity, the dramatic rise in atmospheric greenhouse gas concentrations, and the rise of average global temperatures are now of sufficient concern to lead us to action.

Climate change is apt to affect everyone and everything: food, water, air quality, biodiversity, forests, public health, social order and world peace. It is therefore an issue of great importance for ecological sustainability, social and economic justice, and international diplomacy.

Because the United States uses much more energy per capita than any other nation, our policies to curtail greenhouse gas emissions will be crucial. We must consider not only the kind of fuels used directly but also the energy embodied in all material goods we use. Our nation has long set a standard for others with consequences of past and current behavior.

Involvement by religious communities in education and advocacy will be needed if policies to address global warming are to succeed in politics or in practice in the United States. We unite in urging individual Friends, monthly meetings, and other Friends organizations to seek Divine Guidance in understanding how to:

- reduce our own use of energy and material resources;
- support strong international agreements for reducing greenhouse gas emissions;
- promote national policies for assuring energy and resource conservation;
- participate in a transition to less damaging technologies in our industries, agriculture, buildings and transportation.

These are essential steps to protect life on Earth as God creates and sustains it.

(The Society of Friends' ongoing study of the problem of climate change is described next.)

Friends Responses to Global Change

A Worldwide Consultation among Friends
Introduction to Global Change and the Friends World Committee for Consultation (FWCC)
Prepared February 2010

The first part of this section gives a brief outline of what global change is and what Friends are doing about it. The second part is a brief introduction to the Friends World Committee for Consultation (FWCC).

1. What is Global Change?

Friends around the world are responding to changes in the environment, climate, economy, society. These changes affect us all. They affect us at a practical level and at a spiritual level. Change also affects us all at a global level and in our local communities. Collectively we call these changes "Global Change." One practical example of how global change affects us all and how different changes are inter-connected is the relocation of factories from the developed world, say, Europe or the United States to the developing world. This throws people out of work in America or Europe but increases employment in China or India and leads to lower consumer prices in Africa, Asia, America and Europe. The transfer of manufacturing to the developing world also leads to increased pollution from developing countries and to competition across the world for natural resources, affecting communities in Africa, Asia, Latin America and elsewhere as well as transforming the world economy. All these changes are transforming the world, as we know it. If they continue, the dramatic increases in pollution, deforestation and rapid use of natural resources may fundamentally change the nature of life on earth. Some Friends see these developments as challenges to our fundamental covenants with God. Other Friends see these changes as threatening life on earth as we know it. These changes give rise to both practical and spiritual issues.

When we use the term Global Change, we see it as being the "unity, integration and the inter-connection of all change. Seemingly different or unrelated changes are in fact aspects or facets of a single greater change."[1] We note that all seemingly different or unrelated changes are connected through their role within a greater global system and are thus best described as all being part of a single unified global change. One of the main changes we refer to is the link between development, industrialization, degradation of land, atmosphere and water and the human contribution to environmental and climate change which threatens the very nature of the world we live in. One of the principal challenges the world faces is how to reconcile the mitigation of the causes and impacts of climate change with the right of developing countries to develop.

> [1] Quote from Julian Stargardt, *Friends and Global Change*, FWCC-AWPS, 2008 p.1, available online at www.fwccawps.org

Friends at the 2007 Triennial agreed that global change is a concern of Friends worldwide and approved a Minute on the environment and sustainability. Following on from the FWCC Minute, Asia West Pacific Friends agreed on a Minute, which asked FWCC to consider holding a worldwide Consultation on Global Change to discern if there is a distinctive Quaker voice on global change. FWCC agreed to hold a Feasibility Study and after receiving the recommendations of that Study, agreed to hold a Consultation. The Consultation process is now underway and we invite you to participate. We set out below how you can participate as well as brief information on the Consultation process and brief background on FWCC.

We have yet to hear the voices and experiences of many Friends. In some cases, these are the voices of communities feeling the greatest impact of Global Change. The Consultation is a process designed to offer Friends around the world the opportunity to tell their own stories and share their own experiences of the effects of change, their visions, discernments and the actions they are taking in response. It is our intention to design a process that encourages the participation of previously unheard voices from around the world.

2. What is the Friends World Committee for Consultation (FWCC)?

The FWCC is the Friends' world umbrella body, which links together yearly meetings representing all the different strands of Friends traditions around the world. FWCC sponsors international gatherings of Friends, including meetings of the Committee usually every three years [Triennials] and world conferences and consultations on a periodic basis. This Consultation on Global Change is an example of the type of activity that FWCC convenes.

A small team based in London and headed by the General Secretary, who manages FWCC's day-to-day activities. The General Secretary reports to the Central Executive Committee (CEC), which is composed of Friends from the four geographical sections and at-large members. The CEC meets annually in conjunction with a Section gathering.

The FWCC's world officeis in London and is composed of four Sections, Africa Section, Asia West Pacific Section (AWPS), Europe and Middle East Section (EMES), and Section of the Americas. Each Section is independent and has its own work and activities but works cooperatively with the others.

More information about FWCC can be found on the website www.fwcc.org and more information about the global change initiative can be found at www.fwccglobalchange.org.

FWCC.173 Euston Road, London NW1 2AX. UK Registered charity number 611247

Shinto Faith Statement

This statement was prepared by the Jinja Honcho, the representative body of all Shinto Shrines in Japan. It was printed by the ARC, *Alliance of Religion and Conservation,* and before that, along with statements from ten other faiths, in *Faith in Conservation* by Martin Palmer with Victoria Finlay, published by the World Bank in 2003. (Website: http://www.arcworld.org/faiths.asp?pageID=74

The Kami

The ancient Japanese considered that all things of this world have their own spirituality, as they were born from the divine couple. Therefore, the relationship between the natural environment of this world and people is that of blood kin, like the bond between brother and sister.

> "In the beginning of the universe there appeared various Kami, or deities from the chaos. A pair of male and female deities appeared at the end and gave birth first to islands, their natural environment, and then to several more deities who became ancestors of the Japanese."

An agricultural society based on rice cultivation like that of Japan cannot exist without unification and harmony among all things on this earth: mountains, rivers, the sun, rain, animals, and plants, not to mention cooperation among people. So, it was natural that people developed the idea that they could make their society flourish only when they worked together, fully performing their own role, but at the same time, helping and supporting each other. This gave rise to the spirit of revering various Kami, the land, nature, people, and, on top of that, the spirit of appreciation of harmony among all these aspects of Nature

The Children of Kami

Shinto regards that the land, its nature, and all creatures including humans are children of Kami. Accordingly, all things existing on this earth have the possibility of becoming Kami. Nevertheless, revered status as Kami is limited to those that live quite extraordinary lives beyond human wisdom or power and that have a profound influence, for good or ill, on human beings. As to natural elements or phenomena that have such enormous power, there exist Kami of Rain, Kami of River, Kami of Thunder, Kami of Wind, Kami of Mountain, Kami of Ocean. All these Kami are involved in the life of a rice-cultivating agricultural society.

Speaking of the reverence toward Kami of Mountain, it started with people's awareness of mountains as an important source of water for rice cultivation. Then, people came to regard the mountain itself as a sacred object. This mountain faith prepared the way not only for the preservation of mountain forests but also for conservation of the cycle of the ecosystem, given the fact that mountain forests supply rich nutrition to seas through the rivers, and support good inshore fishing.

In ancient times, reverence toward a holy mountain was expressed by paying respect directly to the mountain itself. Nowadays, Shinto has a building, or a compound of buildings, where Kami spirit dwells permanently, and people worship by performing Matsuri—a festival to offer prayers to Kami—in these buildings.

Matsuri Festivals for Nature

There are many kinds of Matsuri performed in each locality throughout the year. Large or small, these Matsuri are mostly based on the agricultural cycle. Two of the most important festivals each year are the spring festival called Kinensai, a festival to pray for a rich harvest, and the autumn festival called Niinamesai, a festival to offer thanks for the successful harvest.

Shinto

People of each locality have been carrying out these festivals every year since ancient times. In this sense, it can be said that Shinto consists of reverence and gratitude to the land, its nature, and the life that these natural elements give to human beings.

With the reverence of Kami, Shinto spontaneously developed through the way of life of the ancient Japanese. It has neither written dogma nor a teaching book, but people revere numerous deities who are figuratively described as "8 million different deities." A deity with a female form, Amaterasu Ohmikami, is revered most highly among them, but the idea of one absolute god or a hierarchy among numerous Kami has never existed, and still does not. Yet, each Kami has an individual character to which people offer their worship, believing in that as the virtue of each Kami.

> "There exist Kami of Rain, Kami of River, Kami of Thunder, Kami of Wind, Kami of Mountain, Kami of Ocean. All these Kami are involved in the life of a rice-cultivating agricultural society."

Suggestions from Shinto

Shinto regards the land and its environment as children of Kami. In other words, Shinto sees nature as the divinity itself. These days, people often say, "Be gentle to nature" or "Be gentle to the earth." But these expressions sound somehow like the fault of putting the cart before the horse. We feel it is humanity's arrogance. It seems that humans can dominate nature as the master and ultimately "repair" nature, using technical-scientific means. But Kami are the origin of all lives, and the life of all things is deeply connected to them. This leads to an awareness of the sacredness of life and an appreciation for life given by Kami.

From ancient times, Japanese people have faced nature and invisible existence with awe and appreciation. And they used to have a principle: *"to return the thing given to the human as a gift of nature to its original place."* Until the Edo era (1603–1867) this circulation system of Japanese society functioned very well. After that, with the development of modern industry, the level of Japanese life was elevated in material terms, and now people enjoy lives free of want.

But in fact, the Japanese spirituality inherited from the ancient ancestors has been gradually lost or hidden somewhere deep in our consciousness. It might not be an exaggeration if we said that not only environmental problems but also all problems of modern society have been caused by lack of the awe, reverence, and appreciation for nature that ancient people used to have and taught us.

In Conclusion

Environmental issues, after all, depend on our self-awareness of the problems and our determination to take responsibility. We often say that things look different depending upon one's viewpoint.

So, Shinto suggests that we should shift our point of view and look at our environment with the spirit of "reverence and gratitude," that is, with the spirit of parental care for children or with the spirit of brotherhood. And if we can extend this spirit to our neighbors, to our society members, to our country members, to peoples of the world, and to nature, too, transcending differences of thought, ethics, and religion, then this spirit will serve to foster criteria and morals indispensable for keeping our human life healthy.

Threat of Global Warming/Climate Change
2006 Statement of Conscience
From the Unitarian Universalist Association of Congregations (Documents)
Last updated on Thursday, May 26, 2011

Earth is our home. We are part of this world and its destiny is our own. Life on this planet will be gravely affected unless we embrace new practices, ethics, and values to guide our lives on a warming planet. As Unitarian Universalists, how can our faith inform our actions to remedy and mitigate global warming/climate change? We declare by this Statement of Conscience that we will not acquiesce to the ongoing degradation and destruction of life that human actions are leaving to our children and grandchildren. We as Unitarian Universalists are called to join with others to halt practices that fuel global warming/climate change, to instigate sustainable alternatives, and to mitigate the impending effects of global warming/climate change with just and ethical responses. As a people of faith, we commit to a renewed reverence for life and respect for the interdependent web of all existence.

A Matter of Science

There is scientific consensus that the Earth's climate is changing due to global warming/climate change caused primarily by the human use of oil, coal, and natural gas. The burning of these fossil fuels releases carbon dioxide into the atmosphere, which traps more heat from the sun. Global warming/climate change is accelerating as planetary temperatures reach record highs. The melting of polar ice and mountain glaciers may cause sea levels to rise by at least three feet, probably much more, and by eighty feet in coming centuries if the average temperature rises five degrees, warming that will be difficult to avoid. Half of the world's plant and animal species are at risk of extinction by 2100 as habitats are destroyed and ecosystems unravel. The huge Siberian permafrost peat bogs are apparently starting to melt, releasing methane and accelerating global warming/climate change. Antarctic glaciers are sliding into the ocean faster than previously expected, which may result in worldwide coastal flooding. Rapidly melting polar ice caps and glaciers provide visual evidence of global warming/climate change. Indirect effects due to melting polar and Greenland ice can upset the delicate salt balance in the North Atlantic Ocean, triggering a shift in the thermohaline current, which ironically may result in a local ice age in Northern Europe and parts of North America.

Increasing temperatures can devastate human communities and wildlife habitats. Warmer climates are extending toward the poles, dramatically altering ecosystems. Melting polar ice caps raise sea levels and upset the delicate balance of ocean salinity. This imbalance may lead to a shift in ocean circulation patterns, which could wreak havoc with regional climates. Recent increases in sea surface temperatures are linked with more intense hurricanes.

Global warming/climate change can cause both increases and decreases in local temperatures and precipitation. Until now the effects of global warming/climate change have been proportionate to increases in greenhouse gas concentrations. We can minimize the damage of climate change only if we act vigorously and soon—in the next decade according to top climate scientist. Since human-generated greenhouse gases are at a level not seen for at least 600,000 years, effects will persist and increase for a while even as we begin to control emissions. Climatic changes, combined with habitat destruction and pollution, are causing loss of species, forests, human settlements, glaciers, and coastal heritage sites. All living organisms depend on ecosystems that can be sustained only in relatively narrow temperature ranges.

The recent rapid global average temperature increase is indeed the result of human activity. While the climate is always changing, attribution studies using sophisticated supercomputer global climate models show that natural causes do not account for the recent rapid temperature increase and that human activity does. See the 2001 IPCC/SPM report, Figure 2.4.

A Matter of Faith and Justice

As Unitarian Universalists, we are called by our seventh Principle to affirm and promote "respect for the interdependent web of all existence of which we are a part." We envision a world in which all people are assured a secure and meaningful life that is ecologically responsible and sustainable, in which every form of life has intrinsic value. In other words, Unitarian Universalists are called to defer to a balance between our individual needs and those of all other organisms. Entire cultures, nations, and life forms are at risk of extinction while basic human rights to adequate supplies of food, fresh water, and health as well as sustainable livelihoods for humans are being undermined. To live, we must both consume and dispose. Both our consumption and our disposal burden the interdependent web of existence. To sustain the interdependent web, we must burden it less while maintaining the essentials of our lives. Hurricanes Katrina and Rita are painful omens of how racism, sexism, and poverty worsen the effects of global warming/climate change. Our world is calling us to gather in community and respond from our moral and spiritual wealth; together we can transform our individual and congregational lives into acts of moral witness, discarding our harmful habits for new behaviors and practices that will sustain life on Earth, ever vigilant against injustice.

A Matter of Policy

Global warming/climate change is not only an environmental phenomenon; it is a hotly contested policy issue. All countries, in particular developing countries, will be unable to protect their residents from sea level increases, frequent and intense droughts, heavy rains, and violent hurricanes and tornadoes. Species worldwide face extinction from these same events. It is a bitter irony and a grave injustice that economically developed countries that are most responsible for global warming/climate change possess the wealth, technology, and infrastructure to cope with its negative effects, while those who have the least will have the largest burdens to bear.

In 1992, the United States ratified the United Nations Framework Convention on Climate Change. The Convention calls for its signatories to stabilize their greenhouse gas emission rates. It also states that economically developed countries will take the lead in reducing greenhouse gas emissions and not use scientific uncertainty about some aspects of climate change as a cause for delaying an immediate response. While the scientific evidence is solid, there seems to be an effort by some to confuse the public. To date, the United States has not ratified the Kyoto Protocol to the Convention, which sets milestones for reducing greenhouse gas emission rates. International cooperation is critical for addressing this global dilemma.

A Call to Action

Affirming that we are of this earth and that humankind has brought about global warming/climate change, we, the member congregations of the Unitarian Universalist Association, pledge to ground our missions and ministries in reverence for this earth and responsibility to it as we undertake these personal practices, congregational actions, and advocacy goals.

Personal Practices

- Reduce our use of energy and our consumption of manufactured goods that become waste;
- Use alternative sources of energy to reduce global warming/climate change and encourage the development of such sources;
- Choose the most energy-efficient transportation means that meet our needs and abilities (e.g., walk, bike, carpool, use mass transit and communication technologies, and limit travel);
- Determine our personal energy consumption and pledge to reduce our use of energy and carbon emissions by at least 20 percent by 2010 or sooner and into the future;
- Reuse, recycle, and reduce waste;
- Plant and preserve trees and native plants and choose sustainably harvested wood and wood products;
- Eat and serve energy-efficient food that is locally produced and low on the food chain;
- Use financial resources to encourage corporate social responsibility with reference to global warming/climate change;
- Model these practices by committing to a life of simplicity and Earth stewardship;
- Consume less, choose appliances that are rated energy-efficient (e.g., by the EPA Energy Star Program), and choose products and materials that are made from renewable resources and can be recycled at the end of their usefulness; and
- Commit to continue to learn about the science, impact, and mitigation of global warming/climate change and communicate this knowledge by teaching about and discussing the problems and dangers of, and actions to address, climate change.

Congregational Actions

- Celebrate reverence for the interdependent web of existence in all aspects of congregational life;
- Treat environmentally responsible practices as a spiritual discipline;
- Seek certification through the Green Sanctuary Program of the Unitarian Universalist Ministry for Earth;
- Educate ourselves, our children, and future generations on sustainable ways to live interdependently;
- Whenever possible, plan congregational facilities around proximity to public transportation and encourage congregants, as they are able, to travel by public transportation, walking, biking, and carpooling;
- Seek U. S. Green Building Council Leadership in Energy and Environmental Design (LEED) certification for all new congregational building projects and use LEED guidelines for renovation projects;
- Use congregational financial resources to positively address the global warming/climate change crisis;

- Practice environmentally responsible consumption and encourage voluntary simplicity among members;
- Build a broader base for environmentally mindful policies and practices through congregational alliances within Unitarian Universalism, through interfaith channels, and with secular entities; and
- Maximize the energy efficiency of congregational facilities by enrolling in the EPA's Energy Star for Congregations Program.

Denominational Affairs

We call upon our denominational leaders to provide:

- Leadership, by calling upon the major political parties to develop energy and climate change policies and to make them central topics of debate in state, congressional, and presidential elections;
- Education, by providing spiritual, educational, and technical resources for congregational and individual responses;
- Justice, by seeking opportunities for public witness for environmental justice, including joining interfaith and public events promoting a just response to climate change;
- Sustainable practices, by exploring the options for performing environmental audits of all UU properties and for modeling appropriate management and purchasing practices;
- Sustainable investing, by exploring the potential for using the ownership rights of the denomination's financial resources to positively address the global warming/climate change crisis;
- Support, by assisting congregations in evaluating and addressing the risks and challenges they face as a result of global warming/climate change;
- Recognition of congregational action, by encouraging, honoring, and publicizing the work of UU congregations, including those that achieve Green Sanctuary accreditation; and
- Ministry, by recognizing and supporting the need for UU leaders to help others understand the urgency and severity of addressing global warming/climate change, the resulting potential for despair, and places to find hope for the future.

Advocacy Goals

1. Full compliance with the United Nations Framework Convention on Climate Change, with the understanding that because human activity is affecting global climate change, it follows that the greater our total population the greater the impact;
2. Ratification of and compliance with the Kyoto Protocol;
3. Funding for research and development of renewable energy resources and energy-efficient technologies that includes a shift of federal subsidies from fossil fuel industries to renewable energy technologies and improved energy efficiency;
4. Funding of regional, national, and international programs to assist in mitigating the effects of global warming/climate change;
5. Safe and responsible development of power sources with low greenhouse gas emissions;
6. Policies and practices that reduce greenhouse gas emissions and increase forestation and other forms of carbon dioxide sequestration;

7. Funding for development of energy-efficient mass transit and encouragement of its widespread use;
8. Global warming/climate change impact studies (including physical, social, and economic effects) to be conducted by local and regional governments, with the findings to be incorporated into local government processes;
9. Urban and regional planning designed to reduce energy consumption;
10. Access to family planning services in the United States and around the world;
11. Significantly strengthened Corporate Average Fuel Efficiency (CAFE) standards for automobiles and light trucks;
12. National greenhouse gas emissions reduction targets of 10 percent below current levels by 2015, 20 percent by 2020, and 60 percent by 2030;
13. United States policy that takes a leadership role in future global efforts to reduce greenhouse gas emissions and mitigate the negative impacts of global warming/climate change;
14. Monitor, propose, and support legislation at the local and state level related to global warming/climate change and opportunities to reduce emissions; and
15. Provide information on legislative advocacy opportunities to members of the congregation.

Given our human capacity to reflect and act upon our own lives as well as the condition of the world, we accept with humility and determination our responsibility to remedy and mitigate global warming/climate change through innovation, cooperation, and self-discipline. We undertake this work for the preservation of life on Earth.

United Church of Christ

A Resolution on Climate Change
United Church of Christ
(Resolution of Witness)

From the Twenty-Sixth Synod of the United Church of Christ
http://www.ucc.org/synod/resolutions/climate-change-final.pdf [c. April, 2008]

<u>Resolution</u>

WHEREAS, the impact of global warming, as currently predicted and understood by leading scientists and scientific bodies around the world in reports of the United Nations Intergovernmental Panel on Climate Change, as well as in reports of the National Aeronautics and Space Administration and the National Academy of Sciences, will dramatically and negatively alter God's gracious gift of creation;

WHEREAS, the effects of global warming are already clearly evidenced in the melting of glaciers and shrinking of the polar caps, threatening the polar bear with extinction and the Native Peoples of the Arctic with loss of food resources, land, ancient traditions and ways of being in the world;

WHEREAS, experts speak with a profound sense of urgency and clearly state that the window of opportunity to avoid catastrophic climate change is rapidly diminishing;

WHEREAS, global warming will have a disproportionate impact on those living in poverty, least developed countries, the elderly and children and those least responsible for the emissions of greenhouse gases;

THEREFORE, BE IT RESOLVED that the Twenty-Sixth General Synod of the United Church of Christ admits Christian complicity in the damage human beings have caused to the earth's climate system and other planetary life systems, and urges recommitment to the Christian vocation of responsible stewardship of God's creation, and expresses profound concern for the pending environmental, economic, and social tragedies threatened by global warming, to creation, human communities and traditional sacred spaces;

WE FURTHER RESOLVE that the Twenty-Sixth General Synod of the United Church of Christ urges the United States Government to respond to global warming with great urgency and firm leadership by supporting mandatory measures that reduce the absolute amount of greenhouse gas emissions, and in particular emissions of carbon dioxide, to levels recommended by nationally and internationally recognized and respected scientific bodies;

WE FURTHER RESOLVE that the Twenty-Sixth Synod of the United Church of Christ urges state and local governments to support and invest in energy conservation and, specifically, in sustainable, renewable and affordable systems of transportation, and calls on business and industry to lead in responses to global warming through increased investments in efficient and sustainable energy technologies that are economically accessible and just;

WE FURTHER RESOLVE that the Twenty-Sixth General Synod of the United Church of Christ urges all segments of the Church to address global warming in their decisions and investments and in their educational and advocacy efforts;

TO THAT END, the Twenty-Sixth General Synod of the United Church of Christ calls on the Covenanted Ministries of the United Church of Christ, specifically Wider Church Ministries and Justice and Witness Ministries, to address the severe nature of this global warming crisis as one of the most urgent threats to humankind and, indeed, all of God's precious planet earth and that Local Church Ministries develop materials to help churches "green" their buildings.

CANADIAN INTERFAITH
CALL FOR LEADERSHIP AND ACTION ON CLIMATE CHANGE
October 25, 2011

Climate change: the spiritual roots of a crisis

1. We, representatives of Canadian faith communities, are united in our conviction that the growing crisis of climate change needs to be met by solutions that draw upon the moral and spiritual resources of the world's religious traditions. We recognize that at its root the unprecedented human contribution to climate change is symptomatic of a spiritual deficit: excessive self-interest, destructive competition, and greed have given rise to unsustainable patterns of production and consumption. Humanity's relationship with the environment has become distorted by actions that compromise the welfare of future generations of life.

2. Our faith traditions and sacred texts call upon us all – individuals, civil society, businesses, industry, and governments – to consider the spiritual dimensions of the crisis of ocean and climate change; to take stock of our collective behaviour; to transform cultures of consumerism and waste into cultures of sustainability; and to respect the balance between economic activity and environmental stewardship. The November 29 – December 9, 2011, 17th Conference of the Parties to the United Nations Framework Convention on Climate Change (COP 17) conference in South Africa has the potential to be a transition point – where we, as a global community, change how we think and act to address climate change.

Values for a sustainable economy

3. The world's religious traditions teach us to look beyond ourselves – individually and collectively, now and for future generations – as we confront the crisis of ocean and climate change, and to reflect on our choices and decisions. We see people as more than consumers with unlimited appetites. The foundations for a sustainable economy include the values of restraint, cooperation, and reciprocity. We believe we must work together in transforming cultures of self-interest and unprecedented consumption into cultures of justice for all.

4. All religious traditions uphold the nobility of the human spirit, calling on us to seek moderation and service to the common good. Such a vision empowers individuals to take responsibility for relationships with each other and our planet. Indeed, our everyday choices about food, transportation, clothing and entertainment are all practical expressions of what we value. At the same time, disconnections between our professed beliefs and our daily actions indicate our need for personal and collective awareness and transformation. We need to seek coherence between our beliefs and our actions, so that our lives and consumption habits reflect our relationship with the rest of humanity and the Earth itself.

The challenge of climate justice

5. Climate change is a planetary crisis that knows no borders. Some countries are far more adversely affected by climate change than others as they experience major changes in weather patterns. They know the impact of rising seas and erosion of lands, leading to drought or flooding. These countries are most often among the poorest and least equipped to respond.

6. Many countries are suffering from the long-term consequences of unrestrained carbon emissions that damage the atmosphere. We believe all nations need to adopt energy policies that result in actual

emission reductions to a fair and safe global level. Organizations, businesses, and individuals have similar duties to reduce their emissions. For high-income nations such as Canada, justice demands that our governments shoulder a greater share of the economic burden of adaptation and mitigation – first and foremost, because of access to greater means, but also because of an historic role in contributing to its causes. We have a moral imperative to act.

A call for leadership and action

7. We call for leadership to put the long-term interest of humanity and the planet ahead of short-term economic and national concerns. The teachings of our faiths tell us that the best interests of one group or nation are served by pursuing the best interests of all. There is one human family and one Earth that is our common homeland. Climate change is a global crisis and requires global solutions that put the well-being of all people first – especially the most vulnerable. Furthermore, our environment is the natural source of our wealth and the home of millions of species for which we are planetary stewards. How long can we barter this priceless inheritance for the promise of growing economic returns?

8. In our neighbourhoods and communities, in businesses and organizations, we need to change wasteful patterns of production and consumption. This calls for a cultural transformation that brings the values of sustainability to the forefront of public consciousness – and into more responsible practices. We cannot wait for others to act but instead must lead by example. Religious organizations, public institutions, and businesses all have important roles to play in promoting ethical consumption and more sustainable lifestyles and practices in their everyday operations.

9. We speak respectfully to our political leaders, who have been entrusted with authority by Canadians. We ask that you act with due regard for the values of both religion and science, looking objectively on the problems confronting our planet. Climate science points to a future of greater instability and unpredictability, problems that can be addressed by action today. We stand ready to work alongside you to promote a future of security, prosperity, and justice – for humankind, and the whole of creation.

10. As you carry out your responsibilities at the United Nations Framework Convention on Climate Change (COP 17), we urge you to honour the values we have described and adopt the following policy goals:

> In the spirit of global solidarity, take collective action by signing and implementing a binding international agreement replacing the Kyoto Protocol that commits nations to reduce carbon emissions and set fair and clear targets to ensure that global average temperatures stay below a 2° Celsius increase from pre-industrial levels;

> Demonstrate national responsibility by committing to national carbon emission targets and a national renewable energy policy designed to achieve sustainability; and

> Implement climate justice, by playing a constructive role in the design of the Green Climate Fund[1] under United Nations governance, and by contributing public funds to assist the poorest and most affected countries to adapt to and mitigate the effects of climate change.

We believe these to be practical and critical measures necessary to secure the well-being of the planet for future generations of life.

[1] The **Green Climate Fund** is being established by the United Nations to support projects, programme, policies and other activities in developing countries related to climate mitigation and adaptation.

Statement of the 17th Conference of the Parties to the United Nations Framework Convention on Climate Change, December, 2011

Nurture of and respect for Life are central doctrines of all faiths on Earth. Yet today we are endangering life on Earth with dangerous levels of greenhouse gas emissions. These gases are destabilizing the global climate system, heating the Earth, acidifying the oceans, and putting both humanity and all living creatures at unacceptable risk. The extraordinary delicacy of Nature's balance is becoming increasingly apparent, even as human actions inflict ever larger, more dangerous and potentially irreversible changes on the indivisible web of atmosphere, earth, ocean and life that is creation. Today our faiths stand united in their call to care for the Earth, and to protect the poor and the suffering. Strong action on climate change is imperative by the principles and traditions of our faiths and the collective compassion, wisdom and leadership of humanity. We recognize the science of climate change, and we call for global leaders to adopt strong, binding, science based targets for the reduction of greenhouse gases in order to avert the worst dangers of a climate crisis. We urge the nations of Earth to ensure that those who will suffer under climate induced changes such as more severe storms, floods, droughts and rising seas, be aided to adapt, survive and equitably prosper.

We recognize that climate change is not merely an economic or technical problem, but rather, at its core, a moral, spiritual and cultural one. We therefore pledge to join together to teach and guide the people who follow the call of our faiths. We must all learn to live together within the shared limits of our planet. We recognize that just as climate change presents us with great challenges, so too it offers great opportunities. Mitigating climate change can stimulate economies sustainably, protect our planet, lift up the poor, and unite to a common cause people threatened by a common danger. Assisting vulnerable communities and species to survive and adapt to climate change fulfills our calling to wisdom, mercy, and the highest of human moral and ethical values. We commit ourselves to action – to changing our habits, our choices, and the way we see the world – to learning and teaching our families, friends, and faiths – to conserving the limited resources of our home, planet Earth, and preserving the climate conditions upon which life depends. In this spirit, we call upon our leaders, those of our faiths, and all people of Earth to accept the reality of the common danger we face, the imperative and responsibility for immediate and decisive action, and the opportunity to change.

The 17th Conference of the Parties to the United Nations Framework Convention on Climate Change. http://www.interfaithdeclaration.org/index.html

The Durban Addendum to the 17th Conference of the Parties to the United Nations Framework Convention on Climate Change, December 2011

While Climate Change is a symptom, the fever that our Earth has contracted, the underlying disease is the disconnection from Creation that plagues human societies throughout our Earth.

We, the undersigned, pledge to heal this disconnection by promoting and exemplifying Compassion for all Creation in all our actions.

Signed:

Archbishop Desmond Tutu
Bishop Geoff Davies, Executive Director of South African Faith Communities' Environment Institute

Cardinal Wilfrid Napier, Chair of KwaZulu Natal Inter Religious Council
Dr. Mustafa Ali, Secretary General of African Council of Religious Leaders
Bishop Michael Vorster, Methodist Church of Southern Africa, Natal
Rev. Jenny Sprong, Methodist Church of Southern Africa
Rev. Emmanuel Gabriel, Methodist Church of Southern Africa
Stewart Kilburn, HIVAN 911
Saydoon Sayed, WCRP Coordinator, Secretary of KZN IRC
Rev. Sue Britton, Anglican Church of South Africa
Rabbi Hillel Avidan, South African Union of Progressive Judaism
Professor Hoosen Vawda, Nelson Medical School
Cannon Desmond Lambrechts, National Religious Association for Social Development
Dr. Sylvia Kaye, Secretary of Bahai Faith of South Africa
Dhunluxmi Desai, KZN Inter Religious Council and SA Hindu Maha Sabha
Sr. Agnes Grasboek, Sisters of Mariannhill/ World Conference on Religions for Peace
Jerald Vedan, Buddhist Representative for Inter Religious Council
Pundit Raj Bharat, Atman Universal Movement and WCRP
Brasnicck Harting
Fauzia Shaikh
Sr. Usha Jeevan, Brahma Kumaris
Seelan Moodliar, Brahma Kumaris
Ela Gandhi, Honorary President of Religions for Peace
Isaac Withmann, YAGM-ELCA
Kristin Opalinski, LUCSA-LWF
Rev. Lumka Sigaba, Methodist Church of Southern Africa
Jaine Rao, Climate Healers
Sailesh Rao, Climate Healers
Mark Naiker, Catholic Youth
Stuart Scott, Interfaith Declaration on Climate Change
Paddy Meskin, President WCRP SA/ Secretariat for KZN IRC
Moulana Abdullah, IRCPT – Tanzania
Mahomed Yussuf, Sunni Jumait
Maulana Mahomed Ebrahim, Sunni Jamait Ulama
Priscilla McDougal, United Church of Christ
Shamim David, Inter Religious Council of Zambia
Mantanta Wasim, Inter Religious Council of Zambia
Sheikh Idrisa Mtembu, Muslim Association of Malami
Sheikh Saleem Banda, WAMY
Adam Makwinda, World Assembly of Muslim Youth
Fred Kruger, NRCCC

Statement following the 17th Conference of the Parties to the United Nations Framework Convention on Climate Change from the Interfaith Leadership Round Table of KwaZulu Natal:

We, the members of the Inter-Religious community, express our deep disappointment with our local and international political leadership, which has failed to take decisive steps to make the changes required for the survival of humanity and life on Earth.

The science is clear. The influence of greed, materialism and selfishness block the path toward improvement of our physical well-being.

We demand that our political leaders honor previous commitments and quickly move toward more humane, environmentally responsible positions and policies. There is strong evidence that such steps will not be taken in COP-17.

We call on the religious and spiritual communities globally to do what our political leaders have failed to do. We continue to pledge our commitment and encourage all political leaders to stand with us.

We are confirmed in our determination. We will no longer accept words and catchy phrases. We want a commitment to action immediately.

Signed in Durban, South Africa on Wednesday, November 30, 2011 at Diakonia Center.

Namaste,

Sailesh.

—

"Carbon Dharma: The Occupation of Butterflies" at https://www.createspace.com/3722579
Sailesh Krishna Rao, Ph. D., Executive Director, Climate Healers, Inc.
696 San Ramon Valley Blvd. #355
Danville, CA 94526
Ph: (732)-809-3526
+91-9444693341 (India Mobile)
Skype: saileshrao
http://www.climatehealers.org

Peter Eisenhardt

God's Earth is Sacred:

An Open Letter to Church and Society in the United States

(From National Council of the Churches of Christ USA NCCC, February, 2005)

God's creation delivers unsettling news. Earth's climate is warming to dangerous levels; 90 percent of the world's fisheries have been depleted; coastal development and pollution are causing a sharp decline in ocean health; shrinking habitat threatens to extinguish thousands of species; over 95 percent of the contiguous United States forests have been lost; and almost half of the population in the United States lives in areas that do not meet national air quality standards. In recent years, the profound danger has grown, requiring us as theologians, pastors, and religious leaders to speak out and act with new urgency.

We are obliged to relate to Earth as God's creation "in ways that sustain life on the planet, provide for the [basic] needs of all humankind, and increase justice."[1] Over the past several decades, slowly but faithfully, the religious community in the United States has attempted to address issues of ecology and justice. Our faith groups have offered rich theological perspectives, considered moral issues through the lens of long-standing social teaching, and passed numerous policies within our own church bodies. While we honor the efforts in our churches, we have clearly failed to communicate the full measure and magnitude of Earth's environmental crisis—religiously, morally or politically. It is painfully clear from the verifiable testimony of the world's scientists that our response has been inadequate to the scale and pace of Earth's degradation.

To continue to walk the current path of ecological destruction is not only folly; it is sin. As voiced by Ecumenical Patriarch Bartholomew, who has taken the lead among senior religious leaders in his concern for creation: "To commit a crime against the natural world is a sin. For humans to cause species to become extinct and to destroy the biological diversity of God's creation . . . for humans to degrade the integrity of Earth by causing changes in its climate, by stripping the Earth of its natural forests, or destroying its wetlands . . . for humans to injure other humans with disease . . . for humans to contaminate the Earth's waters, its land, its air, and its life, with poisonous substances . . . these are sins."[2] We have become un-Creators. Earth is in jeopardy at our hands.

This means that ours is a theological crisis as well. We have listened to a false gospel that we continue to live out in our daily habits—a gospel that proclaims that God cares for the salvation of humans only and that our human calling is to exploit Earth for our own ends alone. This false gospel still finds its proud preachers and continues to capture its adherents among emboldened political leaders and policy makers.

The secular counterpart of this gospel rests in the conviction that humans can master the Earth. Our modern way of life assumes this mastery. However, the sobering truth is that we hardly have knowledge of, much less control over, the deep and long-term consequences of our human impacts upon the Earth. We have already sown the seeds for many of those consequences. The fruit of those seeds will be reaped by future generations of human beings, together with others in the community of life.

The imperative first step is to repent of our sins, in the presence of God and one another. This repentance of our social and ecological sins will acknowledge the special responsibility that falls to those of us who are citizens of the United States. Though only five percent of the planet's human population, we produce one-quarter of the world's carbon emissions, consume a quarter of its natural riches, and perpetuate scandalous inequities at home and abroad. We are a precious part of Earth's web of life, but we do not own the planet and we cannot transcend its requirements for regeneration on its own terms. We have not listened well to the Maker of Heaven and Earth.

The second step is to pursue a new journey together, with courage and joy. By God's grace, all things are made new. We can share in that renewal by clinging to God's trustworthy promise to restore and fulfill all that God creates and by walking, with God's help, a path different from our present course. To that end, we affirm our faith, propose a set of guiding norms, and call on our churches to rededicate themselves to this mission. We firmly believe that addressing the degradation of God's sacred Earth is *the* moral assignment of our time comparable to the Civil Rights struggles of the 1960s, the worldwide movement to achieve equality for women, or ongoing efforts to control weapons of mass destruction in a post-Hiroshima world.

Ecological Affirmations of Faith

We stand with awe and gratitude as members of God's bountiful and good creation. We rejoice in the splendor and mystery of countless species, our common creaturehood, and the interdependence of all that God makes. We believe that the Earth is home for all and that it has been created intrinsically good (Genesis 1).

We lament that the human species is shattering the splendid gifts of this web of life, ignoring our responsibility for the well-being of all life, while destroying species and their habitats at a rate never before known in human history.

We believe that the Holy Spirit, who animates all of creation, breathes in us and can empower us to participate in working toward the flourishing of Earth's community of life. We believe that the people of God are called to forge ways of being human that enable socially just and ecologically sustainable communities to flourish for generations to come. And we believe in God's promise to fulfill all of creation, anticipating the reconciliation of all (Colossians 1:15), in accordance with God's promise (II Peter 3:13).

We lament that we have rejected this vocation, and have distorted our God-given abilities and knowledge in order to ransack and often destroy ecosystems and human communities rather than to protect, strengthen, and nourish them.

We believe that, in boundless love that hungers for justice, God in Jesus Christ acts to restore and redeem all creation (including human beings). God incarnate affirms all creation (John

1:14), which becomes a sacred window to eternity. In the cross and resurrection we know that God is drawn into life's most brutal and broken places and there brings forth healing and liberating power. That saving action restores right relationships among all members of "the whole creation" (Mark 16:15).

We confess that instead of living and proclaiming this salvation through our very lives and worship, we have abused and exploited the Earth and people on the margins of power and privilege, altering climates, extinguishing species, and jeopardizing Earth's capacity to sustain life as we know and love it.

We believe that the created world is sacred—a revelation of God's power and gracious presence filling all things. This sacred quality of creation demands moderation and sharing, urgent antidotes for our excess in consumption and waste, reminding us that economic justice is an essential condition of ecological integrity. We cling to God's trustworthy promise to restore, renew, and fulfill all that God creates. We long for and work toward the day when churches, as embodiments of Christ on Earth, will respond to the "groaning of creation" (Romans 8:22) and to God's passionate desire to "renew the face of the Earth" (Psalm 104:30). We look forward to the day when the lamentations and groans of creation will be over, justice with peace will reign, humankind will nurture not betray the Earth, and all of creation will sing for joy.

Guiding Norms for Church and Society

These affirmations imply a challenge that is also a calling: to fulfill our vocation as moral images of God, reflections of divine love and justice charged to "serve and preserve" the Garden (Genesis 2:15). Given this charge and the urgent problems of our age—from species extinctions and mass poverty to climate change and health-crippling pollution—how shall we respond? What shall we be and do? What are the standards and practices of moral excellence that we ought to cultivate in our personal lives, our communities of faith, our social organizations, our businesses, and our political institutions? We affirm the following norms of social and environmental responsibility:

Justice: Creating right relationships, both social and ecological, to ensure for all members of the Earth community the conditions required for their flourishing. Among human members, justice demands meeting the essential material needs and conditions for human dignity and social participation. In our global context, economic deprivation and ecological degradation are linked in a vicious cycle. We are compelled, therefore, to seek eco-justice, the integration of social justice and ecological integrity. The quest for eco-justice also implies the development of a set of human environmental rights, since one of the essential conditions of human well-being is ecological integrity. These moral entitlements include protection of soils, air, and water from diverse pollutants; the preservation of biodiversity; and governmental actions ensuring the fair and frugal use of creation's riches.

Sustainability: Living within the bounds of planetary capacities indefinitely, in fairness to both present and future generations of life. God's covenant is with humanity and all other living creatures "for all future generations" (Genesis 9:8-17). The concern for sustainability forces us to be responsible for the truly long-term impacts of our lifestyles and policies.

Bioresponsibility: Extending the covenant of justice to include all other life forms as beloved creatures of God and as expressions of God's presence, wisdom, power, and glory. We do not determine nor declare creation's value, and other creatures should not be treated merely as instruments for our needs and wants. Other species have their own integrity. They deserve a "fair share" of Earth's bounty—a share that allows a biodiversity of life to thrive along with human communities.

Humility: Recognizing, as an antidote to arrogance, the limits of human knowledge, technological ingenuity, and moral character. We are not the masters of creation. Knowing human capacities for error and evil, humility keeps our own species in check for the good of the whole of Earth as God's creation.

Generosity: Sharing Earth's riches to promote and defend the common good in recognition of God's purposes for the whole creation and Christ's gift of abundant life. Humans are not collections of isolated individuals, but rather communities of socially and ecologically interdependent beings. A measure of a good society is not whether it privileges those who already have much, but rather whether it privileges the most vulnerable members of creation. Essentially, these tasks require good government at all levels, from local to regional to national to international.

Frugality: Restraining economic production and consumption for the sake of eco-justice. Living lives filled with God's Spirit liberates us from the illusion of finding wholeness in the accumulation of material things and brings us to the reality of God's just purposes. Frugality connotes moderation, sufficiency, and temperance. Many call it simplicity. It demands the careful conservation of Earth's riches, comprehensive recycling, minimal harm to other species, material efficiency and the elimination of waste, and product durability. Frugality is the corrective to a cardinal vice of the age: prodigality—excessively taking from and wasting God's creation. On a finite planet, frugality is an expression of love and an instrument for justice and sustainability: it enables all life to thrive together by sparing and sharing global goods.

Solidarity: Acknowledging that we are increasingly bound together as a global community in which we bear responsibility for one another's well-being. The social and environmental problems of the age must be addressed with cooperative action at all levels-local, regional, national and international. Solidarity is a commitment to the global common good through international cooperation.

Compassion: Sharing the joys and sufferings of all Earth's members and making them our own. Members of the body of Christ see the face of Christ in the vulnerable and excluded. From compassion flows inclusive caring and careful service to meet the needs of others.

A Call to Action: Healing the Earth and Providing a Just and Sustainable Society

For too long, we, our Christian brothers and sisters, and many people of good will have relegated care and justice for the Earth to the periphery of our concerns. This is *not* a competing "program alternative," one "issue" among many. In this most critical moment in Earth's history, we are convinced that *the central moral imperative* of our time is the care for Earth as God's creation.

Churches, as communities of God's people in the world, are called to exist as representatives of the loving Creator, Sustainer, and Restorer of all creation. We are called to worship God with all our being and actions, and to treat creation as sacred. We must engage our political leaders in supporting the very future of this planet. We are called to cling to the true Gospel—for "God so loved the cosmos" (John 3:16)—rejecting the false gospels of our day.

We believe that caring for creation must undergird, and be entwined with, all other dimensions of our churches' ministries. We are convinced that it is no longer acceptable to claim to be "church" while continuing to perpetuate, or even permit, the abuse of Earth as God's creation. Nor is it acceptable for our corporate and political leaders to engage in "business as usual" as if the very future of life-support systems were not at stake. Therefore, we urgently call on our brothers and sisters in Christ, and all people of good will, to join us in:

Understanding our responsibilities as those who live within the United States of America – the part of the human family that represents five percent of the world population and consumes 25 percent of Earth's riches. We believe that one of the surest ways to gain this understanding is by listening intently to the most vulnerable: those who most immediately suffer the consequences of our overconsumption, toxication, and hubris. The whole Earth is groaning, crying out for healing-let us awaken the "ears of our souls" to hear it, before it's too late.

Integrating this understanding into our core beliefs and practices surrounding what it means to be "church," to be "human," to be "children of God." Such integration will be readily apparent in: congregational mission statements, lay and ordained ministries, the preaching of the Word, our hymns of praise, the confession of our sins, our financial stewardship and offerings to God, theological education, our evangelism, our daily work, sanctuary use, and compassionate service to all communities of life. With this integrated witness we look forward to a revitalization of our human vocation and our churches' lives that parallels the revitalization of God's thriving Earth.

Advocating boldly with all our leaders on behalf of creation's most vulnerable members (including human members). We must shed our complacency, denial, and fears and speak God's truth to power, on behalf of all who have been denied dignity and for the sake of all voiceless members of the community of life.

In Christ's name and for Christ's glory, we call out with broken yet hopeful hearts: join us in restoring God's Earth-the greatest healing work and moral assignment of our time.

Minute on Global Warming and Climate Change

(from World Council of Churches)
Document date: 20.02.2008   Document n° GEN/PUB 05 (extract)

"Be stewards of God's creation!"

"In the beginning God created the heavens and the earth . . .God saw all that he had made, and it was very good"   *(Genesis 1:1, 31, NIV)*

The present minute builds on previous statements of the WCC, especially the statement on the 10th anniversary of the Kyoto Protocol, adopted by the WCC executive committee in September 2007.

The scriptures affirm that the "earth is the Lord's and everything in it" (Psalm 26:1, NIV). In Genesis 1:28, God charges humanity to care for the earth by giving humanity "dominion" over it. The word "dominion" is most appropriately translated as "stewardship", since humanity is not the master of the earth but steward to responsibly care for the integrity of creation. God wondrously and lovingly created a world with more than enough resources to sustain generations upon generations of human beings and other living creatures. But humanity is not always faithful in its stewardship. Mindless production and excessive consumption by individuals, corporations and countries have led to continuous desecration of creation, including global warming and other forms of climate change.

1.   Indigenous peoples all over the world continue to live a respectful way of relating with the environment. The sacred nature of the whole creation is also reflected in different indigenous world-views. While looking at the impact of global warming and climate change, the indigenous peoples' witness provides inspiration and encouragement.

2.   Climate change, as the variation in the earth's global climate or in regional climates over time, and its effects are being experienced already in many regions of the world. Global warming, i.e. the increase in the average temperature of the earth's near-surface air and oceans, is one of the most evident aspects of climate change. The average temperature of the earth is rising. This creates the melting of ice sheets in Antarctica and Greenland, glaciers, permafrost in mountainous regions and the rising of the average sea level. Rising sea levels are already affecting some countries like Bangladesh in Asia and some islands, particularly in the Pacific. A water crisis brought on by severe droughts and unprecedented floods has resulted in a lack of access to safe drinking water and sanitation. Other effects of climate change are hurricanes, cyclones and typhoons, which are increasing in strength, causing loss of life and destruction of the environment and property. Further consequences of climate change are described in the 2007 "Intergovernmental Panel on Climate Change (IPCC) Report". Thus, human life and the whole of creation are suffering a new threat. Climate change raises ecological, social, economic, political and ethical issues, and demonstrates the brokenness of relationships between God, humankind and creation.

3. As stated by the "IPCC Report" and other studies, the situation needs urgent mitigation and adaptation measures in order to prevent further adverse consequences of rising temperatures. Mitigation (dealing with the causes) is a must for developed countries that will have to drastically reduce their carbon dioxide (CO_2) emissions. Adaptation (dealing with the impacts) is urgently needed by developing countries to be able to cope with the changes that are happening. Those who are and will increasingly be affected are the impoverished and vulnerable communities of the global South who are much more dependent on natural resources for their subsistence and do not have the means to adapt to the changes. Deforestation in Africa, Asia and Latin America; the increase in vector-borne diseases (like dengue or malaria) in the higher altitude areas of Africa as a result of the increase in temperature; the forced migration, displacement and resettlement of populations as a result of sea level rise, particularly in the Pacific; are some of the impacts that will continue to increase the pressure on poor and vulnerable communities.

4. To address the threats the world is facing because of climate change, action must be taken now. In December 2007, at the Conference of Parties to the UN Framework Convention on Climate Change (UNFCCC) in Bali, governments agreed on a road map for the negotiation of a new set of commitments under the UNFCCC and the Kyoto Protocol for the post-2012 period. Negotiations are to be concluded by the end of 2009. The United States is now the sole major emitter who has not ratified the Kyoto Protocol. If there is no profound change in life styles, development patterns and the pursuit of economic growth, humanity will not be able to meet the challenge. As the WCC delegation in Bali clearly stressed, "it is our conviction as members of faith communities that a 'change of paradigm' from one way of thinking to another is needed if we are to adequately respond to the challenge of climate change".

5. Climate change is both an environmental issue and a matter of justice. Major green house gas (GHG) emitters have a historic responsibility to assume, to stop and to reverse the current trend. Developing countries, while looking for better conditions for their people, face a dilemma which should be confronted in looking for ways not to repeat the path that led to the present situation. The current unsustainable production and consumption patterns have caused tremendous negative effects in the environment and generated what has been called an ecological debt towards humanity and the earth. This ecological debt can be analyzed in relation to the financial debt. To reverse this trend it becomes crucial to look for technologies and practices both to mitigate and adapt, especially responding to the needs of vulnerable communities.

6. Churches and religious communities can take key leadership roles in addressing global warming and climate change concerns to individuals, communities and governments. The question we must pose is whether we can rise together to meet this unprecedented opportunity. Churches and religious communities, for example, must find ways to challenge and motivate each other to measure our ecological and economic "footprints" and to follow through by making lasting changes in lifestyles and economic pursuits. Church members have to take responsibility for paying their share of the ecological debt

that looms large in the years ahead. Christians should practice "life in all its fullness" (John 10:10) in the face of a modern materialism that has now been globalized. Steps such as these will be a testimony which could permeate societies and be a catalyst for much-needed change.

7. As the effects of global warming can lead to conflict between populations competing over resulted scarce resources, WCC member churches' actions with regards to climate change should also be seen in relationship with the Decade to Overcome Violence and the lead-up to the International Ecumenical Peace Convocation, scheduled to take place in 2011. The theme of the convocation, "Glory to God and Peace on Earth", highlights peace on earth, which should include peace with the earth as well as peace among human beings.

8. Many churches, ecumenical organizations and specialized ministries have already started to take action concerning climate change and global warming. The Ecumenical Patriarch has played a leadership role advocating for the care of creation, involving the scientific community, including its concerns in education curricula and calling, on 1 September 1989, to observe September 1st (the beginning of the liturgical year in the Orthodox Church) as creation day. This call was reiterated by the Third European Ecumenical Assembly, meeting in Romania in September 2007. Also in September 2007, the 9th assembly of the Pacific Conference of Churches called on the churches in the Pacific to advocate for "a regional immigration policy giving citizens of countries most affected by climate change (...) rights to resettlement in other Pacific island nations", and on the global ecumenical family to support this initiative. Forty years after the WCC Uppsala assembly, the Church of Sweden is organizing in Uppsala an inter-religious summit on climate change in November 2008.

The central committee of the World Council of Churches, meeting in Geneva, Switzerland, 13 – 20 February 2008:

A. *Urgently calls* the churches to strengthen their moral stand in relationship to global warming and climate change, recalling its adverse effects on poor and vulnerable communities in various parts of the world, and encourages the churches to reinforce their advocacy towards governments, NGOs, the scientific community and the business sector to intensify cooperation in response to global warming and climate change;

B. *Calls for* a profound change in the relationship towards nature, economic policies, consumption, production and technological patterns. This change is based on the commitment of Christian communities and institutions, including the WCC, which should strengthen the work of the Ecumenical Centre Ecology Group to continue implementing ecological practices in the Ecumenical Centre in Geneva;

C. *Encourages* member churches, specialized ministries and other ecumenical partners to:

a) Share and further develop creative ways of practicing ecologically respectful relationships within the human community and with the earth;

b) Share knowledge and affordable technology that promote environmentally friendly lifestyles;

c) Monitor the ecological footprints of individuals, parishes, corporations and states and take other steps to mitigate climate change and global warming;

D. *Urges* member churches to observe through prayers and action a special time for creation, its care and stewardship, starting on September 1st every year, to advocate for the plight of people and communities of the Pacific, especially in the low lying atolls of Kiribati and Tuvalu, and to find specific ways to show our ecumenical solidarity with those most at risk;

E. *Requests* theological schools, seminaries and academies to teach stewardship of all creation in order to deepen the ethical and theological understanding of the causes of global warming and climate change and of the sustainable lifestyle that is needed as a response;

F. *Promotes* the exploration of inter-religious and inter-cultural avenues for cooperation and constructive response, such as the inter-religious summit planned by the Church of Sweden, ensuring a better stewardship of creation and a common witness through concrete actions.

REFERENCES for the Evangelical Statement:

[1] Cf. "For the Health of the Nation: An Evangelical Call to Civic Responsibility," approved by National Association of Evangelicals, October 8, 2004.

[2] Intergovernmental Panel on Climate Change 2001, Summary for Policymakers; http://www.grida.no/climate/ipcc_tar/wg1/007.htm. (See also the main IPCC website, www.ipcc.ch.) For the confirmation of the IPCC's findings from the U.S. National Academy of Sciences, see, *Climate Change Science: An Analysis of Some Key Questions* (2001); http://books.nap.edu/html/climatechange/summary.html. For the statement by the G8 Academies (plus those of Brazil, India, and China) see *Joint Science Academies Statement: Global Response to Climate Change*, (June 2005): http://nationalacademies.org/onpi/06072005.pdf. Another major international report that confirms the IPCC's conclusions comes from the Arctic Climate Impact Assessment. See their *Impacts of a Warming Climate*, Cambridge University Press, November 2004, p.2; http://amap.no/acia/. Another important statement is from the American Geophysical Union, "Human Impacts on Climate," December 2003, http://www.agu.org/sci_soc/policy/climate_change_position.html. For the Bush Administration's perspective, see *Our Changing Planet: The U.S. Climate Change Science Program for Fiscal Years 2004 and 2005*, p.47; http://www.usgcrp.gov/usgcrp/Library/ocp2004-5/default.htm. For the 2005 G8 statement, see http://www.number-10.gov.uk/output/Page7881.asp.

SIGNATORIES for the Canadian Interfaith Statement

Leaders of faith communities

The Most Reverend Fred Hiltz, Archbishop and Primate, the Anglican Church of Canada

His Grace Bishop Bagrat Galstanian, Primate, Armenian Holy Apostolic Church, Canadian Diocese

Mobeen Khaja, O.Ont., President, Association of Progressive Muslims of Canada

Imam Dr. Hamid Slimi, Chairman of the Canadian Council of Imams, President of Faith of Life Network

Carol Dixon, Presiding Clerk, Canadian Yearly Meeting of the Religious Society of Friends (Quakers)

Reverend Richard E Hamilton, Regional Minister Christian Church (Disciples of Christ) in Canada

The Rev. Bruce Adema, Director of Canadian Ministries, Christian Reformed Church in North America

L.K. (Rev. Fr.) Messale Engeda, Head Priest and Administrator of Ethiopian Orthodox Church of Canada

The Rev. Susan C. Johnson, National Bishop, Evangelical Lutheran Church in Canada

Pandit Roopnauth Sharma, President, Federation of Hindu Temples of Canada

Metropolitan Archbishop Sotirios of Toronto, Head of the Greek Orthodox Church in Canada

The Rt. Rev. Dr. Geevarghese Mar Theodosius, the Diocesan Bishop of North America and Europe

Mar Thoma, Syrian Church

Rev. Willard Metzger, General Secretary, Mennonite Church Canada

Karen McKye, Secretary, National Spiritual Assembly of the Bahá'ís of Canada

Bishop Sylvester Bigaj, Polish National Catholic Church of Canada

The Rev. Dr. H.D. Rick Horst, Moderator of the 137th General Assembly, Presbyterian Church in Canada

The Rev. John Kapteyn, Executive Secretary, Regional Synod of Canada, Reformed Church in America

Brian Peddle, Commissioner, Territorial Commander, Salvation Army, Canada and Bermuda Territory

David Courchene (Nii Gaani Aki Inini – Leading Earth Man), Anishnabe Nation, Eagle Clan, Founder, Turtle Lodge, Sagkeeng First Nation, Manitoba, www.theturtlelodge.org

His Eminence Metropolitan Yurij (Kalistchuk), Primate, the Ukrainian Orthodox Church of Canada

Mardi Tindal, Moderator, the United Church of Canada

Leaders of faith-based organizations

Co-Directors: Jonathan Schmidt/Alice Schuda, Canadian Churches Forum for Global Ministries

Mark Huyser-Wierenga, Chair, Citizens for Public Justice

The Rev. Dr. William Phipps, Chair, Faith and the Common Good

Michael Skaljin, Executive Director, Interfaith Social Assistance Reform Coalition (ISARC)

Mary Corkery, Executive Director, KAIROS: Canadian Ecumenical Justice Initiatives

More endorsing faith communities and faith-based organizations

Rt. Rev. Linda Nicholls, Area Bishop of Trent-Durham & Suffragan Bishop, Anglican Diocese of Toronto

John N. Dorner, PhD, Liaison, Environmental Stewardship, Office of Social Justice, Archdiocese of Ottawa

Claire Doran, Director of the Education department, Canadian Catholic Organization for Development and Peace

Norman Lévesque, Director of the Green Church Program, Canadian Council for Ecumenism

Sister Pat Boucher, President, Canadian Federation of Sisters of St. Joseph

Heather Eaton (Chair), Saint Paul University

Peter Timmerman, York University, Toronto, Canadian Forum on Religion and Ecology

Mary Finlayson RSCJ, President, Canadian Religious Conference

Dr. Gary Groot, President, Canadian Unitarian Council

Rev. Frances Deverell, President, Canadian Unitarians for Social Justice

Ida Kaastra-Mutoigo, CRWRC Director, Canada, Christian Reformed World Relief Committee (Canada)

Ann Broderick, CND, Provincial Leader of the Canadian English speaking Sisters of the Congregation of Notre Dame, Congregation of Notre Dame – Visitation Province

Kesta Occident, Congregational Leader, Congregation of the Sisters of Holy Cross

Fay Edmonds, GSIC, General Superior, Grey Sisters of the Immaculate Conception

Evanne Hunter, IBVM, Canadian Provincial Leadership, Institute of the Blessed Virgin Mary (Loretto Sisters)

Margaret Galbraith, Chair, Interfaith Coalition for Climate Justice, Member, Universalist Unitarian Church of Halifax Social Responsibility Committee

Christine Boyle, Coordinator, Interfaith Institute Justice, Peace and Social Movements (www.interfaithjustpeace.org)

Jim Webb, S.J., Provincial Superior, Jesuits in English Canada

Rabbi Aaron Levy, Founder and Director, Makom: Creative Downtown Judaism

Shahla Khan Salter, Chair, Muslims for Progressive Values Canada

Samira Kanji, President & CEO, Noor Cultural Centre

Suzanne Marshall, OLM, Congregational Leader, Our Lady's Missionaries

Adele Finney, Executive Director, The Primate's World Relief & Development Fund

(Fr.) Paul E. Hansen, C.Ss.R., Biblical Justice Advocacy, Redemptorists Father and Brothers

Jack Lynch, SFM, Superior General, Scarboro Missions

Risa Alyson Cooper, Director, Shoresh Jewish Environmental Programs

Sister Mary Beth McCurdy, Congregational Leader, Sisters of Charity of the Immaculate Conception

Sister Jean Goulet, c.s.c., Regional Animator, Sisters of Holy Cross, English Canada Region

Denece Billesberger, Treasurer, Sisters of Instruction of the Child Jesus, Soeurs de l'Enfant Jesus

Sister Sandra Shannon, General Superior, Sisters of Providence of St. Vincent de Paul

Sister Joyce Harris, ssa, Social Justice Committee Chair, Sisters of St. Ann

James Ramsay, Chair, Social Justice Committee, St. Basil's Roman Catholic Parish, Ottawa

Jacquelyn Morris, Rector's Warden, St. James Anglican, Perth, ON

Cathy Robertson, Chairperson, Outreach/Social Justice Team, St. Peter's Erindale Anglican Church

Rev. Innen Ray Parchelo, Director, Tendai Buddhism Canada

Zul Kassamali, President, Toronto Area Interfaith Council

SIGNATORIES for the Evangelical Statement*

* Institutional affiliation is given for identification purposes only. All signatories do so as individuals expressing their personal opinions and not as representatives of their organizations.

Rev. Dr. Leith Anderson, Former President, National Association of Evangelicals (NAE); Senior Pastor, Wooddale Church, Eden Prairie, MN

Robert Andringa, Ph.D., President, Council for Christian Colleges and Universities (CCCU), Vienna, VA

Rev. Jim Ball, Ph.D., Executive Director, Evangelical Environmental Network; Wynnewood, PA

Commissioner W. Todd Bassett, National Commander, The Salvation Army; Alexandria, VA

Dr. Jay A. Barber, Jr., President, Warner Pacific College, Portland, OR

Gary P. Bergel, President, Intercessors for America; Purcellville, VA

David Black, Ph.D., President, Eastern University, St. Davids, PA

Bishop Charles E. Blake, Sr., West Angeles Church of God in Christ, Los Angeles, CA

Rev. Dr. Dan Boone, President, Trevecca Nazarene University, Nashville, TN

Bishop Wellington Boone, The Father's House & Wellington Boone Ministries, Norcross, GA

Rev. Dr. Peter Borgdorff, Executive Director, Christian Reformed Church, Grand Rapids, MI

H. David Brandt, Ph.D., President, George Fox University, Newberg, OR

Rev. George K. Brushaber, Ph.D., President, Bethel University; Senior Advisor, *Christianity Today*; St. Paul, MN

Rev. Dwight Burchett, President, Northern California Association of Evangelicals; Sacramento, CA

Gaylen Byker, Ph.D., President, Calvin College, Grand Rapids, MI

Rev. Dr. Jerry B. Cain, President, Judson College, Elgin, IL

Rev. Dr. Clive Calver, Senior Pastor, Walnut Hill Community Church; Former President, World Relief; Bethel, CT

R. Judson Carlberg, Ph.D., President, Gordon College, Wenham, MA

Rev. Dr. Paul Cedar, Chair, Mission America Coalition; Palm Desert, CA

David Clark, Ph.D., President, Palm Beach Atlantic University; Former Chair/CEO, Nat. Rel. Broadcasters; Founding Dean, Regent University; West Palm Beach, FL

Rev. Luis Cortes, President & CEO, Esperanza USA; Host, National Hispanic Prayer Breakfast; Philadelphia, PA

Andy Crouch, Columnist, *Christianity Today* magazine; Swarthmore, PA

Rev. Paul de Vries, Ph.D., President, New York Divinity School; New York, NY

Rev. David S. Dockery, Ph.D., Chairman of the Board, Council for Christian Colleges and Universities; President, Union University, Jackson, TN

Larry R. Donnithorne, Ed.D., President, Colorado Christian University, Lakewood, CO

Blair Dowden, Ed.D., President, Huntington University, Huntington, IN

Rev. Robert P. Dugan, Jr., Former VP of Governmental Affairs, National Association of Evangelicals; Palm Desert, CA

Craig Hilton Dyer, President, Bright Hope International, Hoffman Estates, IL

D. Merrill Ewert, Ed.D., President, Fresno Pacific University, Fresno, CA

Rev. Dr. LeBron Fairbanks, President, Mount Vernon Nazarene University, Mount Vernon, OH

Rev. Myles Fish, President/CEO, International Aid, Spring Lake, MI

Rev. Dr. Floyd Flake, Senior Pastor, Greater Allen AME Cathedral; President, Wilberforce University; Jamaica, NY

Rev. Timothy George, Ph.D., Founding Dean, Beeson Divinity School, Samford University, Executive Editor, *Christianity Today*; Birmingham, AL

Rev. Michael J. Glodo, Stated Clerk, Evangelical Presbyterian Church , Livonia , MI

Rev. James M. Grant, Ph.D., President, Simpson University, Redding, CA

Rev. Dr. Jeffrey E. Greenway, President, Asbury Theological Seminary, Wilmore, KY

Rev. David Gushee, Professor of Moral Philosophy, Union University; columnist, Religion News Service; Jackson, TN

Gregory V. Hall, President, Warner Southern College, Lake Wales, FL

Brent Hample, Executive Director, India Partners, Eugene OR

Rev. Dr. Jack Hayford, President, International Church of the Foursquare Gospel, Los Angeles, CA

Rev. Steve Hayner, Ph.D., Former President, InterVarsity; Prof. of Evangelism, Columbia Theological Sem., Decatur, GA

E. Douglas Hodo, Ph.D., President, Houston Baptist University, Houston, TX

Ben Homan, President, Food for the Hungry; President, Association of Evangelical Relief and Development Organizations (AERDO); Phoenix, AZ

Rev. Dr. Joel Hunter, Senior Pastor, Northland, A Church Distributed; Longwood, FL

Bryce Jessup, President, William Jessup University, Rocklin, CA

Ronald G. Johnson, Ph.D., President, Malone College, Canton, OH

Rev. Dr. Phillip Charles Joubert, Sr., Pastor, Community Baptist Church, Bayside, NY

Jennifer Jukanovich, Founder, The Vine, Seattle, WA

Rev. Brian Kluth, Senior Pastor, First Evangelical Free Church; Founder, MAXIMUM Generosity; Colorado Springs, CO

Bishop James D. Leggett, General Superintendent, International Pentecostal Holiness Church; Chair, Pentecostal World Fellowship; Oklahoma City, OK

Duane Litfin, Ph.D., President, Wheaton College, Wheaton IL

Rev. Dr. Larry Lloyd, President, Crichton College, Memphis, TN

Rev. Dr. Jo Anne Lyon, Executive Director, World Hope; Alexandria, VA

Sammy Mah, President and CEO, World Relief; Baltimore, MD

Jim Mannoia, Ph.D., President, Greenville College, Greenville, IL

Bishop George D. McKinney, Ph.D., D.D., St. Stephens Church Of God In Christ, San Diego, CA

Rev. Brian McLaren, Senior Pastor, Cedar Ridge Community Church; Emergent leader; Spencerville, MD

Rev. Dr. Daniel Mercaldo, Senior Pastor & Founder, Gateway Cathedral; Staten Island, NY

Rev. Dr. Jesse Miranda, President, AMEN, Costa Mesa, CA

Royce Money, Ph.D., President, Abilene Christian University, Abilene, TX

Dr. Bruce Murphy, President, Northwestern University, Orange City, IA

Rev. George W. Murray, D.Miss., President, Columbia International University, Columbia SC

David Neff, Editor, *Christianity Today*; Carol Stream, IL

Larry Nikkel, President, Tabor College, Hillsboro, KS

Michael Nyenhuis, President, MAP International; Brunswick, GA

Brian O'Connell, President, REACT Services; Founder and Former Executive Director, Religious Liberty Commission, World Evangelical Alliance; Mill Creek, WA

Roger Parrott, Ph.D., President, Belhaven College, Jackson, MS

Charles W. Pollard, Ph.D., J.D., President, John Brown University, Siloam Springs, AR

Paul A. Rader, D.Miss., President, Asbury College, Wilmore, KY

Rev. Edwin H. Robinson, Ph.D., President, MidAmerica Nazarene University, Olathe , KS

William P. Robinson, Ph.D., President, Whitworth College, Spokane, WA

Lee Royce, Ph.D., President, Mississippi College, Clinton, MS

Andy Ryskamp, Executive Director, Christian Reformed World Relief Committee, Grand Rapids, MI

Rev. Ron Sider, Ph.D., President, Evangelicals for Social Action, Philadelphia, PA

Richard Stearns, President, World Vision, Federal Way, WA

Rev. Jewelle Stewart, Ex. Dir., Women's Ministries, International Pentecostal Holiness Church; Oklahoma City, OK

Rev. Dr. Loren Swartzendruber, President, Eastern Mennonite University, Harrisonburg VA

C. Pat Taylor, Ph.D., President, Southwest Baptist University, Bolivar, MO

Rev. Berten A. Waggoner, National Director, Vineyard, USA; Sugar Land, TX

Jon R. Wallace, DBA, President, Azusa Pacific University, Azusa, CA

Rev. Dr. Thomas Yung-Hsin Wang, former International Director of Lausanne II, Sunnyvale, CA

Rev. Dr. Rick Warren, Senior Pastor, Saddleback Church; author of *The Purpose Driven Life*; Lake Forest, CA

John Warton, President, Business Professional Network, Portland, OR

Robert W. Yarbrough, Ph.D., New Testament Dept. Chair, Trinity Evangelical Divinity School, Deerfield, IL

John D. Yordy, Ph. D., Interim President, Goshen College, Goshen, IN

Adm. Tim Ziemer, Director of Programs, World Relief, Baltimore, MD

ERROR: undefined
OFFENDING COMMAND:

STACK:

Made in the USA
San Bernardino, CA
16 February 2014